ALZHEIME

Mam

A HEAD'S UP ON ALZHEIMER'S

RUTH COLGAN

ACKNOWLEDGMENTS

First and foremost I would like to thank my husband Declan and children Nicole and Paul.

Declan without your continuous love and support I would have never gotten through all the years, you were always my rock and still are. You always put mam first and you never let her or dad down. They were so proud to call you their son-in-law. And I am so proud to have such a wonderful caring generous man as my husband. Thank you for never letting me give up and holding me when I thought I just couldn't keep going. Thank you for not running to the hills.

Nicole, thank you for being the fantastic young lady that you are. You gave so much of your time to your nanny and never looked for anything in return. I know when you lost nanny you felt like you lost one of your best friends but please remember she is always with you and will guide you throughout your life, helping you on whatever career path you choose. You are so clever and kind. Thank you for helping me stay sane, and thank you for reminding me that patience is a virtue.

Paul, thank you for being the most honest grounded person I know. I say person because although you are only a kid you are wiser than a lot of adults I know. Thank you for making me smile and giving me hugs when I looked like I needed them. Thank you for never demanding time even though at times I know you could have done with it. Remember grandad will always have your back and watches out for you all the time.

Audrey, thank you for being you. Without your continued support through all of this I don't know what I would have done. You held me up when I just couldn't do it any more, you played the bad cop when I needed you to. You are one of the kindest and most generous people I know. I am so happy that I have you as my sister.

Mrs Maureen Byrne, Thank you for being my second mam. Your friendship with mam is one I truly admire and hope I have some day. Thank you for being so patient with mam even though at times she was so mean to you. Thank you for being my confidant and my friend. I will always have a special place in my heart for you.

Thank you Margaret, the lovely woman who helped to care for mam at home. Your kindness will never be forgotten

Thank you to all the carers who looked after mam in the nursing home. You are gifted people with very large hearts. And I will never forget how kind you were to mam.

Thank you Uncle Sean and Auntie Susan, who would often take Nicole and Paul at a moment's notice. Thank you for keeping some normality in their lives. And thanks for having a listening ear for all of us. We love you dearly

Thank you May and Tom Colgan, (my mother in law and father in law), without your continued guidance and support I don't know what I would have done. You gave me a much needed ear when I needed it, advice on hand and a hug when I cried on your shoulder. You are two very special people.

Last but certainly not least I would like to thank Beverley Hollowed, author of 11 books herself, without your help I never would have been able to bring this dream to a reality. You gave up your time to help me even though you have lots going on yourself. You are a wonderful lady and I am eternally grateful to my new friend.

INTRODUCTION

Well I don't know exactly where to start. I have decided, rather than just sitting here thinking about mam, I would write about our journey of Alzheimer's and possibly give you a heads up. I would like to say that I am not a doctor, or have any form of medical training, I am not a psychiatrist or an Alzheimer's professional, I am just a daughter and all of my writings here are just my own experiences and observations.

It all started when my dad died, well if I am honest it was probably before then, but I just put that down to a busy mind when mam would forget where she put things, or when she crashed the car because she thought she was going into the village when she was really driving into a housing estate.

Anyway back to the story. Mam was depressed and was being very forgetful, after seeing her doctor it was decided that she should attend the memory clinic in St James's Hospital, they did a few memory tests which signified that she might have a problem with her memory, they gave me a 30 page questionnaire that had to be filled in. Whilst filling it in I quickly realised that there must be a big connection between Alzheimer's and depression, as most of the questions asked about how often mam

1

talked about dying etc. Etc. And at this stage that was very often. All she wanted was to be with my dad.

The memory clinic organised mam to have an MRI of her brain done. The results came back; mam had hydrocephalus of the brain (fluid on the brain). She had a blockage that ironically looked like a map of Ireland, and it was preventing fluid draining from the brain and causing pressure. So therefore it caused confusion as to what was causing mams problem, was it the hydrocephalus or was it Alzheimer's.

They suggested that mam should get the fluid drained but mam was not having a bar of it." There was no way they were cutting her open at this stage in her life". They were not even sure what exactly could be achieved from this. It might bring back her memory or it might make her a whole lot worse a whole lot quicker. There was also a very big chance she may never come out of it alive. Mam choose to stay as she was and try to enjoy her life as best she could. None of us were quite sure about this decision but it was mams wish and we had to respect that decision. To be honest I really don't think she ever understood any of it. She just wanted to get the hell out of the hospital. Afterward any time we would bring her for her appointments, she would get so mad, wondering why on earth she was there when there was nothing wrong with her. I often wonder now what we were doing there, it never helped, no-one ever came back with any suggestions of how to deal with this big change in our lives. They just gave her some pills and sent us on our way with a check- up appointment.

After a few more MRI's of her brain they noticed mams hydrocephalus wasn't getting any worse but her memory was still deteriorating, so although mam was never officially diagnosed with Alzheimer's they assumed that was what it was.

I remember one day driving with my children, Nicole and Paul, and mam down to a shopping centre. She looked at me very seriously and said "There is something wrong with me, what is it love?" I tried my best to explain to her that she had Alzheimer's. She started to get upset. I told her not to worry we were going to be with her every step of the way.

That evening myself and my husband, Declan, went to dinner with my brother in law Sean and sister in law Susan. I started to chat about mam and stated there was no way I was going to be able to do this. Sean gave me the foot in the behind I needed and said "of course you are, you don't have a choice you just have to get on with it ". His honesty kicked me into touch I was going to do this not only because I had to but because I wanted to.

We were going to have a long road ahead of us. There would be tears and tantrums but there would also be love, happiness and laughter. Laughter is a word not often associated with Alzheimer's. It's like the forbidden word. Alzheimer's is not funny, you are right but funny things do happen in the course of it and I'm just saying that it is ok to laugh at those moments.

At this point I would like to offer my 1st piece and possibly my most important piece of advice: If you can possibly get your loved one to give you enduring power of attorney, please get it sorted it will save you so much heartache down the line. Go visit your solicitor and get it done. It will allow you to make the hard decisions when your loved one no longer can do it for themselves. So now that is said on with the story I go.

ON HER TRAVELS

Shortly after being diagnosed, mam headed over to my sister, Audrey, in Florida. It was a trip herself and my dad had made many times together, now she was going alone. I would have loved to go with her but with work and family commitments it was out of the question. I also knew it was only on the flight she would be alone and Audrey would be there the other end. And once Audrey had her I knew she would be just fine. I appreciate it's a long flight but it felt like days until I finally got that call from Audrey to say she had her. It probably seems a bit of an over-reaction but something was telling me this was going to be a fast rollercoaster. I was right.

One day, while Audrey sister went into the office for an hour, my mam thought that it would be a good idea to go for a walk to get some milk. Now that would be fine if Audrey's house wasn't in the middle of the countryside. It might take a few minutes before you would see a car and the nearest shop was about a 15-20 minute drive. Out she headed walking in the direction of the shops. A short while later,(we are not exactly sure how long later as mam told us this part) but a large jeep pulled up beside her and inside was a gentleman and his son. They told mam it was too hot to be walking these roads and she shouldn't be walking alone, so they offered her a lift. By the grace of god they were genuine people and they dropped her to the shop. During this time Audrey frantically phoning the house but no one was answering so she came home. When she found no mother she was worried sick. She looked around hoping to find some note, some clue to find out where she might be, there was none. She jumped into her car and called my nephew, Keith, who was also on his way home and told him the story. They both started on their search. Audrey finally found her walking back through a "not so nice "neighbourhood. Audrey could have killed her and kissed her both at the same time, she choose the latter. She explained to mam how dangerous her actions had been but mam just told her she was being ridiculous that the people who had picked her up were lovely and she shouldn't be so negative.

I wish I could say that she didn't try this again but sadly she did. Again she took off to go to the shops this time she walked the whole way but at the last stage took a wrong turn and ended up at a different set of shops which she didn't recognise. She went into a dollar store to cool off and started looking around. She looked confused enough that a lady asked her was she ok. Mam told her that she wasn't sure. The lady asked mam did she know where she staying. Mam told her she didn't know the full address but pointed in the direction of Audrey's house and said she'd recognise it when she saw it. The lady and her husband offered mam a lift home. She took it. Thankfully yet again she made it home safe. I still reckon to this day that my dad sent those people to mind my mam because god knows this could have been where my story ends. Mam didn't try it again for the rest of her holiday, which was a relief for everyone. She came home just after New Years' relaxed and happy.

She stayed in a lot when she came home, I appreciate it was the winter but that had never stopped my mam before, I began to worry about her general wellbeing. She came down with a couple of colds but other than that she got through the winter quite well and my worries were in vain. In spring she decided she would visit my other sister, Viv, in France. I helped her pack and brought her to the airport. Again it was going to be a wait until Viv called but at least time it wouldn't be so long. I got the call a whole lot quicker than that. The airline called to say they had mam in the airport; she had fallen asleep at a different gate and had missed her flight. They said they had called her lots of times over the tannoy but mam had not heard it. Declan raced out to the airport to collect her as I was collecting the children from school. He arranged for a flight for the next day for her along with some airport assistance to make sure she made the flight ok.

The next day she did just that and Viv called to say she had her and that she had brought her home to her house. Another house in the countryside. Mam was having a wonderful time and stayed put until one day she decided to take my niece off for a walk in her pram. Another search party ensued when she didn't return after an hour. They found them both safe and well besides mam giving out stink that no one spoke English "what kind of country doesn't speak English??" Was her only response.

Mam returned home after a few weeks. She looked great with a lovely colour on her face. She had really enjoyed her stay. I'm sure many people are reading this wondering why on earth we had let her go to these places. In hindsight we shouldn't have, as I reckon now it made her worse a lot quicker. Not being in her own environment had confused her. But mam loved to travel and we were in denial.

I spoke to my sisters and we all finally agreed mam was getting a lot worse. And unfortunately her travelling days were over unless one of us could be with her at all times.

THINGS CAN CHANGE VERY QUICKLY

They say Alzheimer's is a long hall, and the sufferers have long periods at the same level and then go downhill a little at a time. Well mam rewrote the book on this, she went downhill on roller-skates. As the months went by mam repeated herself more and more. She would have just told you a story to only tell you again 10 minutes later. She would forget where she put things for example, her handbag, her best friend and neighbour, Maureen, spent most of her life looking for it. We discovered mam liked to keep lots of things under her mattress or base of her bed, so if you are looking for paperwork or a pair of earrings or maybe just some missing sweets, have a little look you never know what you might find.

We had many different hurdles to get over with mam, each one presenting itself at different times. One of those times was when we realised that mam was a danger to herself. She had been at mass and we went to collect her after to go out for some lunch. As we were heading out of the church she told me she had forgotten her keys so I said we would stop by the house to pick them up. When we got in through the front door I got a major smell of gas. I ran into the sitting room only to discover mam had dismantled the front of the gas fire and had left it on. I then went into the kitchen to discover she had left on the gas cooker (gas but no flame). We opened the windows and doors straight away. When I said it to mam she just said "oh did I?" There was no panic, no sense of the danger she could have been in. It was then and there I realised we had hit another stage of this horrible disease. So next day Declan had arranged for someone to come in and disconnect the gas. He had an electric fire put in place of the gas fire (just for the light effect). He got rid of the gas cooker and bought her a new electric cooker, not that she cooked, as I bought the ready- made meals in Aldi and microwaved them for her, but for my siblings when they came home to visit. He moved all switches and fuses and hid them from sight so mam couldn't mess with them. It worried me like hell wondering what was going to happen next.

I didn't have to wait long. One day whilst going to her women's club (they went there to play bingo and have a chat) mam spotted us on the other side of the road from her and without even looking she walked straight out onto the road. I started shouting telling her to stop but she just shrugged her shoulders and kept walking. When she reached us, unharmed thank god, my children, Nicole and Paul told her she could have gotten hurt or killed. She told them not to be so silly she was fine. My thoughts …. Oh Crap, She no longer had a sense of danger.

When you went into mams house (PA- Pre-Alzheimer's) she would always offer to make you a cup of tea and a sandwich.

Now though you got a teabag in a cold cup of water and would be given a green mouldy sandwich. No matter how many times I would empty the fridge of the foods that had spoiled, she had her own stash and that was what you got. I would spend hours looking for that stash but I may as well been looking for a needle in a haystack. I never used to say anything to her about the tea just make my excuse to go into the kitchen and make a real cup.

I noticed mam wasn't eating properly, she was picking at the microwave dishes and those she didn't pick at she threw out to the wild cats in the garden, not realising it would bring mice and it did. We caught them all, cleared the place of mice droppings. After a thorough clean I arranged for the meals on wheels to deliver to her each day. She would receive a bowl of fresh soup, a dinner and a dessert which would change daily. She argued with me, stating she was well able to cook for herself and did not need this but I lied and just said that if came for free and sure why wouldn't she take it as she worked all her life for it. She swallowed this (forgive the pun) and eventually gave into the idea and accepted it. I have to commend the meals on wheels service, it is a fantastic option. A fantastic deal, at a very reasonable price.

I went into mam one morning to find the house had been turned upside down. Her bedroom was like a tornado had struck. Every wardrobe had been emptied and every drawer pulled apart.

There were clothes, shoes, photographs, some of my father's ashes; "yes you heard me right My Dads ashes" you name it all over the floor and bed. I even found the sandwich stash that she used to give me to eat, why did I not think to look in the bedroom what kind of idiot was I? I took to cleaning her room putting everything back where it belonged (sandwiches in the bin finally) made the bed and hoovered. All the time mam was looking over my shoulder saying she had been looking for something but couldn't find it. When I asked what she was looking for she had no idea what I was talking about. She said she was cleaning her room.

I honestly think more of my dad ended up in the hoover than in his urn. She would often take out a little bit of his ashes from his urn and put them in a locket only to lose the locket and I would have to replace it without her knowing. Talk about spreading someone's ashes, my dad is in Florida, France, Finglas, Town or in some dump somewhere. As time went on mam would put him into little bottle tops or little boxes that jewellery come in but he would not stay there for long we would find bits of him were often swept up from the floor or drawers and put into the bin. Thank god he is finally at peace now in my house, no more being scattered about.

This "cleaning" that mam did happened every 2nd or 3rd day after that. I would go up to find kitchen or sitting room was "being cleaned" but she never got it finished. At the time there were a lot of burglaries around the area and I used to joke that if they ever came into my mams they would turn right back around as they would think it had already been done. I need not tell you this was exhausting. I found that I was snapping at my own children if they left anything around, purely because I was so tired of cleaning up. Only to have to apologise for being so horrible and that it was not their fault. This too would be an everyday thing, apologising for taking out my frustrations on my own family. As this stage continued and with a bit of research I realised that it could be that, her eyesight was blurry and she couldn't necessarily see what she was looking for, she may also have had a buzzing sound in her ears which made it very hard to concentrate. I'm not sure if the buzzing noise was going on, I have been told since it may have been an issue, but she would never say.

I had to get rid of some of the excess stuff somehow. An idea came to mind. Mam would very often go into Maureen for some tea and watch old movies or listen to music. Mam loved these nights and often lost track of time. I explained to this wonderful lady what my plan was. While mam was busy in her house, my family and I loaded 5 x 80litre boxes with the loose photograph's, documents and the tons of brand new greeting cards (she had a thing for collecting greeting cards) and loaded them all up into the attic. This way it would minimize the amount she could throw around. I also loaded her off season clothes into vacuum pack bags and put them into the attic also. We hid them in the furthest corner of the attic as mam did not like to walk around up there. It worked a treat.

I have to be honest I was sooo glad when this stage moved on bit.

The summer flew by. The children and I put together a little vegetable patch for her. We planted lettuce, scallions, cabbage and rhubarb. Mam had always loved the garden. She had always planted flowers and growing her own little bits and pieces had brought her so much joy in the past. Unfortunately it did little for her now. She had lost almost all interest in it. So instead we would just sit with her and the children would tell her lots of different stories which she soaked up like a sponge, smiling and laughing with them.

Mam would often get her shoes mixed up and would head out with an odd pair on. So we just matched up her usual shoes, then elasticated the rest in pairs and hid them. It was whilst doing this I noticed mams shoes were beginning to slope on one side. So I watched her walking. As she did she was constantly leaning to one side. When we went to the doctors for her check-up I mentioned it and the doctor said it is more than likely caused from the hydrocephalus. A change in her "gate" (the way she walked) was a common occurrence

Autumn came and went without much incident if I rightly remember. Then came the winter.

CHRISTMAS

Mam would always try to help, even climbing up the Stira (attic ladder that pulled down) to get down the Christmas tree. Thankfully she never noticed the stashed boxes. She tried to put the tree together but god love her the top was in the base and she could not figure out how it was so small , she thought she had a bigger tree than that. We got the tree up and decorated it. I put the lights on a timer so as she would not have to fiddle with them. I had them turn on so early in the day because I knew if she did not see them lit when it would be dusk, she would start fiddling, and trust me that is one thing you do not want her to do.

The tree looked lovely and the house finally looked Christmassy. She was so happy the look on her face would remind you of a child. Little did I know at the time how childlike she actually was. I came up the next day delighted with myself that it was all done and was pleasantly surprised to see the house still in order when I came in. I went in to check on the tree to find mam had decided to do some extra decorating of her own. I obviously had not done it as she liked. We had extra decorations of, socks and underwear on the Christmas tree. A bra, hanging from one branch to another, with a little Santa sitting in each cup, as if it were a hammock. We had artificial flowers from a vase in the tree also. All I could do was laugh. When she had gone to kitchen to make me my cold tea, I removed the extra décor and put them away. This was going to be my new routine for the Christmas period, new additions to the Christmas tree every day, some days it would be clothes other days, cutlery, depending on what she would find. Have to admit I found the whole thing very funny. My kids used to get a great kick out of finding the new decorations, it became our daily game.

Christmas was approaching fast and I had bought presents for everyone for mam. I wrapped them up and left them under her tree. Silly mistake, firstly I spent a week looking for them (she had hidden them) when I found them they had been unwrapped but she didn't do it must have been someone else. I was about to learn about the invisible people that lived in mams, no one ever saw them but they got blamed on everything, if something was missing, messed up or was any way questionable it was them not mam that did it. So getting back to Christmas, after rewrapping the presents I put them under the tree again and begged her to leave them there. She did It's just they were re wrapped about 20 times before the children eventually opened them on Christmas day and acted surprised as they saw the gifts.

My 2 sisters, brother Ger and their families came home that Christmas. Viv and her family and her dog stayed with mam while, Audrey and her family stayed with me and Ger stayed with his in-laws, unfortunately it was very Christmassy.. No room at the inn, we were packed to the rafters but thankfully Ger is easy going and didn't mind. Still it was an exciting time. The week went by in a blur. Christmas dinner was hectic but fun, trying to squeeze everyone in it was like playing Tetris. The children laughed, played and some just hung out. The adults talked of times gone by whilst enjoying a glass of wine and mam loved every minute of it. She loved the house being busy and noisy. Although, she would get a little agitated if she was out of her house for too long and would only settle down again when she was back in her own surroundings. I reckon something happened to her in the early stages and maybe she got a little lost somewhere but eventually found her way back but the fear of it happening again was inside her head never to leave, not that this was necessarily a bad thing , it was keeping her from wandering.

I did have to warn Viv though, to hide her valuables as mam would forget someone was staying and she would wander into their rooms and take some of their stuff and put it somewhere, the place we liked to call "the black hole". All sorts of things went missing, but mam never saw them or touched them it was the invisibles again putting them into that black hole. This new habit never changed, anyone that would stay in mams would have to mind their valuables and quite a lot of things did go missing over that year, only some were found when we were clearing out her house. Vivs' children found this a little difficult.

Their nanny would constantly take their stuff and when they would find it, mam would claim it as her own. This was very confusing to them as they had never seen their nanny like this. But with a bit of explaining they got it, just like dealing with a baby, wait until she put it down out of her hands then you can reclaim it as yours.

Mam point blank refused to go out without her hat. She would demand to have it before she went to mass and would cause havoc until she did. This was made very difficult when the hat went into The Black Hole. I have to add we never did find the black hole or mams favourite hat. One day whilst at the shops Viv came across a similar one and just said to mam "oh look what I found". I never thought it would work but she didn't even notice as we handed her the impersonator. She put it on her head and off she went. I went back to the shops and bought 3 more exactly the same in case the hat went missing again.

It's a Christmas I will remember for all time as we had quite an eventful one (eg the kids flooded the bathroom and the ceiling leaked right onto the beautifully laid out Christmas dinner table) but I wouldn't change it for the world. It was a fantastic week but sadly it came to an end and everyone had to go home. It was "Just US" again.

It came to the time when the tree had to come down and mam was not impressed, she did not understand why it could not stay up, she loved it and the lights. This became our daily battle, I'd say yes she said no way until one day, in February mind, I came up to the tree gone. I decided I'd better look for it, so I could make sure it was put away for next year. I found it alright, half was thrown in the garage, with lights and baubles and nickers still on it, the other half was in the box room in the house. I need not tell you it took me 2 days to eventually sort it all out and put it away.

A NEW YEAR SO NEW SITUATIONS

It was very cold and mam kept going over to the post box or out into the garden at all hours of the day and night. It was very nerve racking but I was so grateful that my mam had such amazing neighbours, one in particular, that they kept a very watchful eye over her. Before going to bed each night Maureen would walk out into the garden and have a look at mams house to make sure all looked right. It's so important to have some kind of backup, I appreciate that this is not always possible but it certainly helps.

Ever since my dad died, I bought my mam a bunch of flowers every single week to cheer her up. She loved the flowers so much so, that the flowers I bought were not enough and she would love to go into the garden and pick lots of branches from her bush, it had lovely yellow flowers on it but not exactly what you would pick. She would proceed to put these branches into the vase with the flowers I had bought almost suffocating the poor things. I would find the place walking in bugs and earwigs, all from mams lovely flowers and dare you say anything about them.

Once a week we would go up to the local shopping centre and I would buy mam and my children an ice cream. She loved nothing more than to sit on the seats and watch the world go by. Talking to anyone who looked in her direction telling me she knew them from years ago and just couldn't quite remember their name. I copped on real quick not to argue with her about knowing them as she would be very upset and angry with me. I knew it was just the confusion of the whole thing but I learned very early on that the worse thing I could do was to disagree with her. You see mam became very clever in hiding her loss of memory when it came to people, she would say hi to everyone, in case she was meant to know them. And if she said "oh you're ….. Or that's ….." And they said sorry "no you must be mistaken" mam would respond with "well you are the image of them" and bless they would look nothing like the person. She would tell total strangers that her husband had died and she was all alone. This became a big bone of contention between us. I had to try to change the subject very quickly or say things like yes but there are people with you all the time. I was terrified someone would be listening to her and follow her home.

Mam loved to have a chat with just about anyone. Some people take advantage of this, my experience was The Jehovah Witnesses. You have to understand my mother was an avid catholic and went to mass every week and went every day during lent. Mam told me one day that this lovely girl from the church had dropped in to see her and she had a lovely chat and a cup of tea with her. She went on to tell me this same lady was coming up later on in the evening to take mam to a nice meeting where she would meet lots more friends and have a nice cuppa. I made a mental note to be there when this "lady" was due to call up, and we went about our little shopping trip as planned. When I was dropping mam home I found a note had been left by this "lovely lady" from The Jehovah Witness, saying she would be up to collect mam at 7pm. I tried to explain to mam that these people were not from her own church but a different one. It made her so nervous and scared. What would she do when they called? I told her not to worry I would sort it out. Thankfully there was a phone number on the letter So I called this number and politely, well maybe not, told this lady that if she ever stepped foot over my mother's doorstep, she would live to regret it. She tried to argue with me but trust me she got my message and never showed up again. I personally have nothing against Jehovah Witnesses but there was no way anyone was converting my mam at this stage in her vulnerable life.

Mam was also very naive, she never used to be, she was always as sharp as a tack but this horrible disease changed all that. An example of this was when some lads from the travelling community called at the door to clear the cobble locking of weeds. Mam agreed to have it done. I swear to god I think my dad used to take over my car and drive it to mams when he knew she needed my help because on that day I decided to call back up to see my mam, (I had seen her an hour ago). When I got there she was all happy. She said she was getting the lads to do the pathway. I asked her how much it would cost. She replied €2.50. I had to laugh I explained to her that it couldn't have been €2.50 that maybe it was €250. Bless, she started to panic saying she wouldn't have that sort of money. I told her it was fine that I would sort it out. She looked at me and said "but I signed something". So I took to ground running. These lads were still in the estate trying to drum up business. I went to the chap and asked how much it was, he told me €250. So again I politely, not so, explained that mam would not be needing his services to which he was not best pleased. I demanded the document mam had signed and spouted out a whole of crap how it wasn't worth the paper it was written on etc. Etc. He was reluctant to hand over the paper but when I took out my mobile and said it wasn't a problem we would call the Gardaí and get them to sort it out. He couldn't give me the paper quick enough. Another lesson learned. At this stage Declan was looking into putting cctv all over my mams to keep her safe, or at least let us be able to keep an eye on her all the time.

MAMS LITTLE CHANGES

But another problem had arisen, Mam was becoming a bit of a story teller. So trying to work out the truth from the lies became a problem. She would tell me people had called telling her that her house was up for sale and they wanted to look around, or some lady called and she gave her a coat because she didn't have one the list goes on and on. Maybe some of these stories were true, most were in her mind but I had to answer with a response that I knew she would like. For example she often told me that she had had a party the previous night with lots of her friends and I would just ask if they had a good time.

In my opinion there is no sense in arguing with someone who has Alzheimer's. They may be at a different point in time in their mind and it might be a better time than this, so who am I to tell her she is wrong. Just because it makes me feel better trying to help her remember, all I am really doing is making her feel more confused and angry because it is different from what is in her mind. I found that agreeing with her would keep her relaxed and happier. I also found that changing an answer would help too. If mam looked as though she wasn't happy with an answer I had given her I would quickly change it and continued to do so until I reached the answer I knew she was happy with. In the beginning I used to forget to do this but quickly learned.

Sometimes If we had a little disagreement, I would walk out of the room, go to the bathroom and return with a smile on my face and say "Hi mam, how are you?" In a happy voice because she would not remember we had argued or even what it had been about but if I had stayed she would go into a quieter and angrier place in her head and could stay there for quite some time not knowing why.

She would get very angry and say dreadful things. One person who got this in the neck all the time was Maureen. Mam would be simply awful to her at times, she would accuse her of taking things or sayings things that this lady would never dream of doing or saying. This lady was like my second mam, I could vent to her and vice versa. We were all on this journey and all we could do was learn as we went along and not give up. I thanked god for her every single day. Maureen found a solution to one of these problems, if mam got upset she would put on music, like Dr Jeckle she turned straight away into Mr Hyde... or whatever way that goes, anyway she would completely calm down and just start singing along to the songs. Amazingly enough as mam forgot words or the names of things, one thing she remembered right to the end, was the words of her favourite ballads. Again later on I discovered the part of the brain that stores music is one of the last things to go. Mams vocabulary had decreased so much, it was like playing Pictionary but instead of drawing it she would describe it or try say what it was used for, for example, she would say " those things you put on your feet"... answer: slippers or shoes. At one stage I was contemplating making a board game called The Alzheimer's head wrecking game.

Mam had started to have a problem with dressing herself. She would often put on 2 tops or maybe 1 top but inside out or back to front. She often put her trousers on over her pj bottoms. I'd come in to find her looking like the Michelin man all dressed up in layers and layers of clothes. One time she had even used a T-shirt as a pair of pants. I seriously thought I was going to die laughing. I had notices a big bulge hanging out the back of mams trousers only to discover it was the t-shirt. She had managed to get her legs into the arm hole and had pulled it up, it must have been so uncomfortable. When I told her she just laughed and started to strip off, this is where the loss of her inhabitations came into play. Not a bother to her to strip off right there in the sitting room and walk upstairs in her birthday suit. Thankfully she didn't do this too often. She did try it once when Declan was sitting there, I never saw him move so fast.

IN NEED OF ASSISTANCE

It was at this point I admitted I needed help. I felt like such a failure, I felt like I should be able to do more but I just couldn't. I went to the doctor to ask for some. I was wondering should I take my mam to live with me and my family in our house. She advised me that I would probably be divorced in the year and I really had to think of my own children and dangers that may present them. She did recommend I ask for some home help from the HSE.

So off I went to my local Healthcare clinic to speak to the public health nurse. This was no easy fete as these ladies and gents are rushed off their feet and are very often out of office, So I basically camped outside in my car waiting for her to come in, I didn't even know what she looked like but every time a member of staff came in, I went right back to reception to ask was it her. I think they got fed up with me asking so they just called her and arranged a time for me to meet her. I did and to my surprise she turned out to be a lifeline. She agreed to come and assess mam. She came and asked mam a lot of questions. Mam was not too pleased that I was not allowed to help her answer them. She would repeatedly say that she was 70 something years old and how was she supposed to remember, Just wait until we were her age. The nurse asked mam 10 questions to which mam got about

5-6 right. The Public Health nurse agreed I needed help and put together a great package for me.

I would have someone who would come in for an hour in the mornings to help mam dress and give her, her medication and breakfast. Someone would come back in the afternoon for a ½ hour to heat up mams dinner and then again ½ hr in the evening to give mam her meds, her tea and help her get ready for bed. It was an absolute godsend and the lady they sent was such a wonderful and understanding person. She put up with mams mean words and unwillingness to be helped and never once complained.

Mam was nice some days and other days very uncooperative saying she didn't need anyone, she had me. I tried to explain that this was to help me also, that is when she turned on me and said "well I don't need anyone I can look after myself". This was very hard for her to understand as she had been such an independent women , In her P.A. (Pre Alzheimer's) years she had worked, cared for 5 children, been an amazing wife, putting up with crap I personally would never have, and kept a lovely home. She paid all the bills and made sure we had everything we needed. In my eyes she was a bit of a wonder woman. So for this lady having a carer made her feel useless. I have to say her carer never did anything to make mam feel this way and would often hide the fact that she was putting on a wash for her etc. Once she even brought home mams soiled bed sheets so mam would not feel bad not being able to wash them.

Mam had begun to hate the washing machine (she broke 3) she would put stuff in them, then because she thought it had been on for hours (it would only have been a few minutes) would decide to turn it off and open it, only to flood the kitchen. Or on another occasion she had put in her bra, after a while she noticed one of the straps sticking out and thought she had to pull it out (note the washing machine was on spin at the time) it was hilarious to watch. Again as I said earlier you have to laugh at the little things that happen during The Alzheimer's years because if you don't you may well find yourself in a straitjacket rocking back and forth trying to find a happy place. (I do not wish to offend anyone by the straight jacket remark and apologise if I've done so).

She would tell people she hadn't seen me in weeks. Thank god everyone who knows me knew better. I discovered why she thought she hadn't seen me. It took me a while but I realised mam did not know who I was anymore, she thought I was just a carer. This was one of the hardest pills to swallow. My mam didn't know who I was any more, now what was I going to do? If I'm honest I got quite upset with this new information I found myself very emotional and normally I wouldn't be a big "crier" (I'm a bit emotionally disabled). I was at the doctors one day and when she asked after my mam I broke down (never done before) but she told me it was completely normal that I was grieving for my mam. She understood mam was not dead but I was grieving for the woman she once was and I was now caring for a woman who looked like my mam but that she was different. This made complete sense to me. I finally understood and could deal with it better. I soon realised my mam actually thought Nicole who was 9 at the time was me. Mam was now living years ago in her head and I had to remember this. This new information was a huge help as I could now play along with her memories of years ago, even learn a few things about her that I didn't already know.

MONEY PROBLEMS

The next big thing was money, I was always nervous when she would go out on her own as she would go to the bank-link and take out a wad of money. I would find this money shoved in her pockets or in her purse. She would put €50 notes into the church envelope (I'm sure they didn't complain). Once we were in the village and she saw a little girl that had just been at her 1st day in school. Mam quickly went to her purse and took out €10 and told her to go buy sweets, I tried to tell mam it was too much but she wasn't having a bar of me (my mam was one stubborn lady when it came to telling her what to do mind I guess I don't lick it off stones) but, thank god, the little girls mammy wasn't a greedy person and made her daughter give it back. I gave mam €1 to give to her instead, which she did and was happy with this.

Mam was hugely generous, to a fault if I'm honest. Once, mam saw a girl standing at the bus stop who seemed upset. Mam went to her and asked her what was wrong. The girl said she had missed the bus and was now going to be late for work and she would be in trouble. Mam gave her €50 and told her not to be upsetting herself and to go get a taxi, which the girl did. Shame on her I say.

It was great living in a village where you know a lot of people, I have a lot of friends who work around and who would have children going to school, so I had a lot of people who would look out for my mam and knew they would look after her should they see anything that was not quite right. An example of this was my friend, Cora, telling me of the wad of money my mam had in her hand and she put it into mams purse and zipped up my mams bag and distracted her long enough that she forgot about it. Mam would often hand people €50 note for a slice pan and ask them was that enough. Thank god the people she encountered were as kind and honest as they were. All these little things were adding up and I knew I had to think of a solution. I offered to take her bank card and suggested I take the money out in case someone was watching her as I didn't want anything to happen to her. She agreed and I would take money out once a week for her. This was great for a while until she would say to me "I've no money, you need to get me money, what are you doing with my money??? I want my card back" I would inquire as to where the money I gave her was gone, I'd get a reply of " I don't know, I didn't touch it" I gave mam her card back once and while I was with her she tried to use the bank-link, only to discover she couldn't remember her pin. This was my chance I helped her out then stored the card away. She eventually asked me for her card back so I gave her an old one I had found in the house. (Mam had about 5 of them as she kept losing them and had to get new ones). This worked a treat, I would take out some cash for her, change it into small denominations and put it in her purse. I would then tell her she had been to the bank already and had taken out her money. I know this sounds really mean, like as if I was confusing her more but it really wasn't, if you ever saw a person standing at a bank link that has forgotten their number, it was panic stations and she would be upset that she couldn't remember, this little lie kept her happier and safer.

I thought it might help if I brought my mam with me to do her shopping, so she would have no need to go to the shops by herself. It was hilarious she would load the trolley with tons of stuff she didn't need, and rather than argue I would let her only to take it back out when she wasn't minding. One of these items was Ham, I found she had a thing for Ham, she would buy packet after packet of ham, no idea why. We would get home only to find she had about 10 packets in the fridge and probably about 5 more stashed away in the cleaning press, bread bin or god only knows where else. She would just say "ah sure I forgot I bought some already and I fancy a ham roll with my cup of tea". She would also buy Wurthers sweets. She would munch away at them all day long. Like a little child you would find stashes of empty wrappers everywhere, in her pockets, shoved down the side of the couch even in her bed. She would crunch and crunch breaking every tooth, how she still had any teeth left amazed me.

I had a surprise call from the public health nurse requesting a visit. So we arranged a time and day and she came loaded with a folder. She sat and asked mam her usual 10 questions, which at this point mam could only answer about 4 correctly. She was surprised at how quickly mam had deteriorated. She explained that her visit had been to try to take some hours away from me but after speaking to mam and seeing how she had gone downhill she said there was no way she could possibly do this and if she could get me any further hours she most certainly would. She did say she would arrange for an Occupational therapist to come visit and He may be able to help with mams living arrangements and also arrange for some living aids to help us. She also said I should start looking into funding for nursing homes.

It was around this time I discovered that mams "filter" was gone. When I say filter I mean you know that thing in our minds that prevents us from saying some terrible things to other people, well mams was gone. We were talking to an old friend of hers in the shops one day, and mam turned to her and said, "god you've put on tons of weight since I saw you last". I was mortified all I could do was apologise to the lady "who now had a lovely red face". Or if mam saw someone looking at an item of clothing in the shop she would say that it was disgusting and how could anyone want to buy it. I would just usher her on as quickly as possible.

My most embarrassing "Filter-less" time was when the Occupational Therapist (O.T) dropped by. He was a lovely gentleman from Zambia. The whole time he was there my mam kept saying "I'm sorry I don't understand your language." He was so kind and just laughed it off. After apologising profusely, He said not to worry he was well used to it.

NURSING HOME SUPPORT SCHEME – (FAIR DEAL)

I started looking into how to go about getting someone into a nursing home and the cost etc. This I have to say was harder than looking after mam. No one actually sat down with me and explained exactly what I was to do which made it very difficult. I will try to keep this as brief and as straightforward as possible and please note my experience is for a widow, so No Spouse, because the figures and other information may change if there is a spouse involved:

1: A: You have to apply for State Support: this is a large form (12 pages to be exact) Form NHSS1, which will include all details of your loved one. You will need to know lots of information for example: a: Details of Medical card - b: details of all income- c: details of all money that goes out - d: details of all cash assets -e: non-cash assets for example a house. From this you will be assessed and told how much the state will pay and how much you have to contribute. You will have to provide statements and documentation to back up everything on this form.

The form states:

"You will have to contribute up to 80% of your income and 7.5% of the value of any assets per year. The HSE pays the

37

balance of your cost. For example: If the cost of care was €1000 per week (PW) and your contribution was €300 PW. The HSE would pay the balance of €700 PW.. " The HSE nursing home section works this out from the information you provide them. If your loved one has No assets (ie: cash or non- cash eg. A house) this means you basically give the home 80% of their pension (I have to say again this is in relation to a widow (No Spouse). I tried the citizens advice bureau and they helped a little. To be honest I just read and re-read and re-read it and worked it out until I got to grips with it. But if you want to you could get legal advice on it. I just never thought of it at the time.

B: you need to Apply for a Care Needs Assessment (often called CNA) appointment. This is also on the form NHSS1 (Section 2)

C: Decide if you would like to apply for the Nursing Home Loan otherwise known as (Ancillary State Support). This loan can be applied for if your loved one owns a property ,basically, instead of paying your full weekly contribution from your own means, It can be collected from the value of the house after your loved one passes away or if you sell the house. I had to get a written valuation done for this but I'm not sure if that is still the case.

2: You then have to have the Care Needs Assessment (CNA) done. This assessment identifies if the person needs long-term nursing home care. It is done by a HSE professional (eg a nurse who is appointed by the HSE, Doctor etc) My mam had hers done by a Geriatrician

3: Once the CNA and the financial assessment are done the HSE are supposed to write to you. I never received that letter or call and it wasn't until I called them myself that I received an answer. They tell you if you are eligible for the State Support (A) and if you applied for the Nursing Home loan (C) they will tell you if you are eligible for this also.

4: You can then go onto the HSE website which lists all of the nursing homes (private, public, voluntary) that have been approved. Make a list of your favourites and visit them. . (We did this step while we were waiting on funding approval 2nd time around)

I cannot state how important it is to check out all the homes you are interested in. Some specialise in Alzheimer's patients. Make sure you have a list of questions you want answered, for example, Are there any additional charges (some homes charge an additional fee per month which is not covered by the HSE.) Do they do the laundry?, are they shared rooms ?,sample menus ? Visiting hours ? I could go on and on. You can also google some questions to ask, there are plenty of great sites on there. I personally needed to make sure the place was spotlessly clean and I looked at the other residents to see if they looked happy. I also dropped in at an unarranged time after, just to make sure it was all ok and not just for show. This is your loved one you are leaving in the care of others, so take your time and choose well, and do your research.

5: If you are happy with a home, put your loved ones name down and if you have been approved, make sure the home is aware that you have been granted funding. The nursing home is supposed to assess your loved one to see if they can meet the requirements that may be needed. This does not always happen in my opinion. We put my mams name down and told them we were still waiting on word from HSE. This helps you to get a little bit ahead as there is often a long waiting list in most nursing homes.

6: If there is a place available you will hopefully be offered it and the nursing home arrange the release of funds with the HSE and you arrange the balance with the home. That is if you have only gone for the state support and not the home loan option.

In my case:

I filled in the application form, attached all the relevant documentation and sent it into the HSE for review. The application was approved but we did not need the funds right there and then. I just wasn't 100% ready for mam to go into a nursing home I was going to stretch every minute I could before I would have to do it. I was left under the impression by the HSE that this funding was fine to be on hold and I was just to call when the time came. This I later discovered was not to be the case. More about that later.

The details above were correct as of December 2013. These could well have changed since.

A LITTLE ANGEL STEPS IN

At this point my mam was completely incontinent. She would have several accidents a day and mams carer was fantastic. Between us we spent quite a lot of time cleaning down walls, doors etc. Making sure everywhere was hygienically clean. But we were in a stale mate with mam having a wash, it was even very difficult to get her to wash her hands sometimes. She would insist she had had a bath or shower and there was no way she was having another one. So as you can well imagine smells do not go away with a quick splash of water so we had to come up with a plan. Nicole was already miles ahead of us. She told her nanny that she wanted to be hairdresser and could she please practice on her hair. All Nicole, had to say was jump and my mam said how high. So at Nicole's request my mam jumped up and said "of Course". So our Thursday night ritual began. When no one was looking, or when I was so busy fussing around, an amazing bond had been building between my nine year daughter and her nanny.

Nicole and I would go up to my mams. Nicole would fill the bath and put in all sorts off wonderful lotions and potions creating fabulous smelling bubbles, she would put her nannies pyjamas and towels on the radiator to warm them. She would call for her nanny and mam would run up the stairs like a big child. Nicole would help her nanny strip, sometimes mam would sing the stripping song "Da da da da.Da da da da" you know how it goes, and would laugh all her way into the bath. Nicole would lower her down into the bath in her little remote control bath seat (best ever provided by the local O.T). Then she would proceed to put on a show for mam while she was in the tub. It could be singing, acting, jokes, the list was endless. Then she would wash mam and wash her hair. I was never allowed to help, as my mam would cause blue murder if I did and this ritual was an absolute necessity. It was wonderful to watch the relationship they had, giggling and laughing like two school girls. Nicole would take her nanny out of the bath dry her, dry her hair and dress her in her pyjamas. She would then tuck her nanny into bed. I was allowed to bring up a cup of tea and a scone.

One evening Declan and Paul decided to drop in to say hi. My mam was in the bathroom upstairs and they were coming in the front door as she was descending the stairs. She stopped suddenly, frozen on her spot and a fearful look came across her face. She said "who is that man with Paul, I don't know him". We reassured her and explained it was my husband and she relaxed a little. I turned to Declan, who was crestfallen by the way, and said well "I guess you're in my club now "the forgotten ones"".

I would like to say that it didn't bother Declan, but it really did. He was heartbroken. He had brought my mam to all of her appointments and had dropped in every other day to have a cuppa with her and now he was forgotten.

A DOWN-TURN

The public Health nurse called and made an appointment to see mam. She arrived and did her 10 memory questions. I think mam only got 2 right. I knew by the look on her face that I was not going to like what was coming next. Because mam had deteriorated so badly it was time to look into nursing homes. I knew this moment was coming but had dreaded it. How would I ever be able to move my mam from a home she loved to a nursing home? But for mams safety and wellbeing I had to put aside my own personal feeling and start with the rest of the nursing home process.

As instructed by the public health nurse I arranged for mam to go see a geriatrician in Blanchardstown Hospital. Mam hated every minute of being there she again kept saying there is nothing wrong with me. I tried to make the time go by quicker and more smoothly by singing with her. My mam had a fantastic voice but now when she got a song in her head she kept singing the same song over and over. But I kept her spirits up and got through the appointment. It was also the geriatricians view mam should be in a nursing home.

I felt like I was being ganged up on, the feeling I was letting my mam down was so overwhelming. I know they were only doing what was best for mam but it was my mam. I finally swallowed back the tears and asked how do I take my mam out of her home? She said mam was at the point where her home could be anywhere as she probably didn't even properly recognise it as her home anymore. A memory came straight to mind of the previous Christmas. My mother in law had invited my mam to come down to her house Christmas night. We brought her and she soon kicked off her shoes and relaxed. She turned to me and said "go into the kitchen there and get these people some sandwiches". She got up, found her way into the kitchen and started looking in the fridge and in the presses. When I asked her what she was looking for she told me her tablets. I had to explain to her that it was not her house, to which she laughed and said "well it feels like home". That memory served me well as it gave me hope. We left the hospital and headed home.

As mams illness progressed she was losing weight and was not so steady on her feet. She would often say she wasn't hungry. Even when one of her favourite dinners was served up to her she would often just say "yuk I hate …" She was losing her appetite but I had to make sure she was still getting enough vitamins and minerals to keep her healthy. So off to the doctor I went, who at this stage knew every little detail of my mam and mams folder was huge. I found it very important to keep an ongoing relationship with mams doctor, just for my own piece of mind.

She gave me a prescription for Ensure drinks. Mam took to these quite well and she would drink it quite happily. But this didn't help with mams unsteadiness. I don't know if she was ever dizzy, she never said, but I would often see her sway and lose her footing. She would insist she was just fine. I mentioned it to the doctor who checked her over and was always fine. It was only later on, we discovered her blood pressure would often dip quite sharply for a couple of minutes but would go back to normal just as quick. So it was very hard for any Doctor to diagnose this unless they were watching her 24-7. One morning, while thankfully, Audrey was with her, she had like a little seizure. Audrey said it all happened very quickly and she shook a little and was out of it but then came back around just as quick.

We called the doctor an explained what had happened, she told us that the quickest way would be to have mam seen in a private hospital. They would do all sorts of blood tests, give her an overall check-up and would do an MRI. That was the clincher we needed to see if mams hydrocephalus had gotten worse. So we got our referral letter and off we went.

We got an emergency appointment and they agreed to see mam by the end of the week. The day arrived and off we went to have her tests done. Now when mam left the house she was like a child on a long journey, full of questions. "Where are we going? Did I do something wrong? When will be there? Did I do something wrong? What are we going to do? Did I do something wrong?

Bless her; my heart went out to her. We were greeted by a lovely nurse who showed us to a day ward. The look on mams face when we walked in, she looked terrified. We asked her to sit on the bed but no way, she would sit in a chair. They came and offered mam some tea and toast to which she declined. They started with tests very quickly, blood tests, blood pressure, a chest x-ray, an MRI and tons more tests that I can't even remember. Everything looked fine. We compared her MRI to previous ones and there was no change. Therefore we had no answers. No reason as to why she had that seizure. They offered mam some lunch to which she replied "No thank you I will have some when I get home". She quite clearly stated that there was no way she was staying there and continually asked "when are we leaving?". After everything was reviewed we were sent on our way with no more information than when we walked in.

MAM'S FALL

Audrey had only gone back a few weeks when one morning my mam had a fall. That morning I had had a phone call from mams neighbour to say mams heating was not working again. Unfortunately mam used to mess with the heating and would often turn it off unknowns to herself. Declan said he would call up straight away and have a look. He got there about 9am and sorted it for the time being but he felt like it might need a service so he called the boiler man. He could have someone out at 12.00 noon that day. Declan called me with the details and told me to make sure I was there when the lad arrived. Mam was fine when Dec left the house at 11am but when I got there at 11.45am I found my mam lying on the floor. My first thought was to Thank God because even if she had fallen straight after Declan left she had only been there 45 minutes, she had not been lying there all night. At least I had some help (the boiler man) he was able to help mam up. She was not screaming in pain or anything, and in hindsight I should not have moved her. But she was begging me to get her up off the floor, so I did. She kept saying she was fine but could not remember how she fell or how long ago it had happened. She said someone had knocked on the door and wanted to buy her house and she tried to get away from them and thinks that's when she fell. I called 999.

Two big strapping ambulance men came through the door and mam greeted them with the biggest smile. "Ah look who has come to see me "the lads laughed and said sure why wouldn't they drop into her. They got her to stand with their support and figured nothing was broken as she would be screaming in pain if it was. But they took her to the hospital for an x-ray just in case.

Well the A&E has never had such excitement as when my mother was there. She started singing like she was having a ballad session at a party. She would give her noble call to someone else to give her a couple a verses. To my surprise mam was in good company and soon her fellow patients were happily singing along. One or two would embarrassingly say that they couldn't sing but my mam wouldn't hear of it. "Of course you can", she'd say "I will help you, what song do you know?" I would ask mam to quieten it down a little that there was sick people here, I did this more for my own embarrassment than anything else, she would just sing louder and tell me sure they are not dead yet it might cheer them up. I had to laugh. The ambulance men waited with us until mam got a wheelchair which took about an hour mind. They didn't care they were having a great time with my mam. I still to this day think of those 2 guys, they were gentlemen with such big hearts, they never judged my mam or got upset with her, they just made her smile.

Mam was watching all the different people being pushed around in wheelchairs and said I would love one of them; I wouldn't have to walk anywhere you could just push me and then laughed her head off as if it was the best joke ever. When mams chair eventually arrived she was delighted, imagine delighted, but she was "I have my own wheelie bin now "she said. Tears were in my eyes from laughing. She waved goodbye to her knights in shining armour with a promise of a cuppa for them when she saw them again.

She was taken into the triage nurse, who checked her over. Mams blood pressure was high. I explained about mams situation and told her that there was no point in asking mam anything, as she would say everything was fine and wouldn't tell the truth. Because first and foremost my mam was a lady and would never want to put anyone out but she also wanted to get the hell out of there so if she fibbed and said she was grand, she might get out quicker.

They sent her down to have an x-ray on her femur and her pelvis then we waited for the consultant to come back with the results. Turned out mam had cracked the neck of the thigh bone and needed an operation. You could have knocked me over with a feather. Here was a woman with a cracked bone and needed a plate put in her leg to fix it and she had been standing up and singing.

They took bloods and did an ECG. We spoke to the orthopaedic doctor who said mams operation would entail a screw, a plate and her leg may end up a little shorter. Mam laughed her head off at this and said "ah sure I will be Hop along Cassidy now" (this used to be my dads' nickname when he had married my mam). I sat and took in all the information, mam lay on the bed and had a little nap. We were waiting a few hours for mam to be brought up to a ward. It was an interesting time. So picture this, a room with white walls, a sink, a chair and a bed but mam was seeing something completely different. She would turn to me and say "they look like lovely apples on that tree, will you pick one for me". My answer would be of course I will. It was here in this whitewashed room I realised mam had hallucinations and could have been having them for quite some time.

After my legs died sitting there, I got up to move to the other side of the bed. Mam had closed her eyes for a moment and when she opened them again she said "Ah, it's great to see you, thanks for coming in " I just laughed and said " sure I couldn't leave you in here on your own" She smile and said "Thanks love"

REPLAY THE HSE APPLICATION SCENE

I knew I had to bite the bullet and relook at the nursing homes. Before I started I called the HSE to make sure everything was all ok only to be told no it wasn't, that due to an outstanding life loan mam had (a release of equity from her home years ago) and the valuation of her house, we would no longer be eligible. I have to say that was almost the straw that broke the camels' back. I think I must have sat there for about an hour crying, wondering how on earth was I going to pay for my mam. Mams release of equity (life loan) which was €40,000 was now going to cost approximately € 105,000 which was to be paid on her death or if we sold the house.

I called the HSE again and was told I would have to re-apply for just, the state support and I would have to come up with the balance each month or sell the house and have her financials reassessed. I knew mams savings would not be able to sustain this additional cost for long but what option did I have. Our problem was we were not allowed the home loan because of the life loan. But when it came to having just the state loan, mam had a non-cash asset (her house) and the life loan was not treated as an outgoing payment. So we were stuck between a rock and a hard place.

Audrey would come home to help me out, at least 3/4 times a year but this year was an exception. She was back and forth so often that I'm sure she thought she lived here. She is one of the kindest, honest, caring people you could ever meet. She always had my back from the start to the end. If I was ever in doubt about decisions I had to make for my mam I would talk to her and we would come up with solutions together. She is also one of the toughest, sharp tongued people you could ever meet, especially when it came to protecting my mam and me. This was really great as when I felt too weak to fight she would always step right up to the mark and deal with it. It was cool that for the period she was home, I could play good cop while she took on the role of bad cop when it came to fighting for mams wellbeing. It also gave me some well needed family time. We could enjoy being a family knowing my mam was being well cared for and most importantly, Safe

While she was in hospital we set about the whole HSE nursing home support scheme (Fair Deal) application Again. We refilled in the form, got up to date statements and documents and brought them down to the HSE office ourselves. We even asked to see a staff member, so they could check and make sure everything was ok. It was and we were told that they would let us know the outcome. Audrey and I then started the long haul of looking for a suitable nursing home. We arranged appointments and visited all the homes that were close enough so I could visit every day. We asked a million questions and checked every nook and cranny to make sure it was suitable for mam. Some were too clinical for me, others needed to be updated.

When you walk into an Alzheimer's unit of a nursing home don't be surprised if you see some strange things. Just remember this may not be what it seems at first glance. It might be just a resident's way of expressing themselves at that time and may have nothing to do with the care that is being received.

Finally we found the perfect one but there was a waiting list as long as my arm. We put her name down and we also put her name down in another one just in case.

MAMS STAY IN HOSPITAL

The operation would take place in two days' time. She was brought up to a ward. She settled in quite quickly which I was surprised at. I explained that she would have to stay here a while and she was ok with this.

Two days flew by and mam went down for her operation. It was a success. Only problem was mam did not understand why she couldn't get up and come home. I explained this about 100 times that she had to wait until she was better. She would get very upset with me and would repeatedly ask "what have I done wrong?" It would break my heart every time she would ask.

One day, on my visit, mam had another little seizure, the nurses came running. She came around a couple of minutes later. They quickly checked her blood pressure and she had had a rapid drop. So this was the cause of her little seizures. I shivered as I thought of how many times this may have happened to her when no one was around. I felt so guilty.

By this stage Audrey had returned from Florida. I didn't know how she was managing to keep returning for me, I know it was with great difficultly, but I sure was grateful that she was there. Viv had come over from France to visit my mam. Mam was delighted with all the attention and my sisters would have her singing and laughing from the morning until the evening. I'm sure the nurses must have hated us. They would get all the ladies all riled up with singing and the likes. Viv would happily help mam's "new neighbours". She would run around all the elderly ladies, refilling their water jugs and rinsing out their drinking glasses.

They moved mam to another ward because there was no way she was going anywhere in a hurry. They put her in the old part of the hospital. It was scary, I could quick easily imagine ghosts roaming the corridors at night. Mam didn't like this part so much. It was darker and generally gloomier but my sisters kept her spirits up. Viv made a new friend, the lady next to mams bed. We reckoned she had Alzheimer's also. As she would ask Viv where she was, and was her family coming to visit. She was also a bit upset because... Her story ….someone was accusing her of stealing the money but she didn't. She wouldn't do that and would Viv help her to prove she didn't do it. She kindly told her it was ok, she would help. That was enough for the lady, she would settle down and ask when was it tea time??? This happened on an hourly basis. It was like watching a part in a movie then rewinding it and watching it again. This is a very common occurrence with Alzheimer's; you kind of feel like someone keeps pressing the rewind button.

We noticed mam was struggling to see. She would often say "ah look at that little girl" when it would be a grown woman, although maybe on the short side. We worked out that she was only seeing shadows and guessing the rest. When you looked into mam eyes her pupils were tiny. They were only about the size of a pinhead. We said it to the nurses but they said it was ok it could be down to her medication but they would say it to the doctor. Unfortunately no matter how long we hung around we never got to see the doctor to get a response.

Christmas was approaching fast and the hospital was the last place we wanted mam to be, so Audrey got to work. She found out that mam could be moved to a much nicer place not too far away in Marino. It was a unit that the hospital owned and was often used for an interim. She could be housed here until we got her a spot in a nursing home.

Before we moved her there though we had to sign The CSAR (Common Summary Assessment Report). Seemingly it's the report that the practitioner has to fill in which is compiled of the CNA (Care Needs Assessment) report and other information. This was the 1st and last time I had ever heard of it. I just signed it with the hospital social worker and hoped it would move things along. They had reaffirmed that mam could not go home. They had done another couple of tests and they had never had anyone score so low and still living at home. It might sound silly but I was actually was quite proud of this; I had kept my mam safe in her own home for as long (and beyond) as possible. They handed us a list of vacancies in nursing homes but none fit. I gave her the names of my top 2 and off she went.

I was grateful at the fact that now mam was actually out of her house that I would not have to put her through all the confusion and upset of packing her up and moving her out. I found this was the way it was going to be, call it divine help or my dad looking out for her but all I know is that when it came to the hard pushes I had a little extra help.

Viv had to head back to her family in France and Audrey's time here was running out fast. This just made Audrey more determined to get mam into that unit. She must have called the lady in the unit at least 5 times in one day and the same the next. They were waiting on a space for her. They were hoping one would come up in a couple of days. Well Audrey was making sure no one else got that room. Her persistence payed off .We got that magical phone call. There was a place in the unit. Even as I write this now tears well up as I remember the relief that, that phone call brought. She was going to be somewhere nice for Christmas.

Just before they moved her, myself and Audrey visited our 1st choice of nursing homes. We spoke to a wonderful lady and explained mams situation. She understood our plight and asked us to leave it with her for a short while. Our hopes were rising, maybe we would not have to move mam into the respite, maybe she could come straight here. She contacted us later that afternoon and asked us to drop in. We rushed down, hearts in our throats. She had a spot so if we could just clarify that the funding from the HSE was in place we were good to go. We called the HSE straight away but we were informed it hadn't been completed yet and they could not give the go ahead. Our hearts sank, we dragged our heels back inside to explain that we would have to leave it. We couldn't believe it, so close but yet so far. This lovely lady did inform us that they had a sister home in Kilcock, and that if mam moved to there she would be given 1st refusal of a bed in our 1st Choice. We left feeling deflated but at least mam wouldn't have to stay in the hospital she would be moved to the new unit in Marino.

ON THE MOVE

They moved mam out of the hospital straight away. The place was lovely, so bright and airy. Lovely view of the gardens and everyone was so nice. We brought up a few of mams things. She no longer had to spend all day in bed in her pjs. They would encourage patients to get up, help them dress and would even have a lovely dining area for them to eat their meals. Mam was very impressed with the tablecloths and little vases, with flowers, on each of the dining room tables. Audrey could go back to America happy, knowing mam was in a nice place.

I received a call from our 1st choice nursing home. They still did not have a place but there sister home in Kilcock had one coming up. I hadn't seen this place so Declan and I went to have a look. It was a lovely place with a specialised Alzheimer's unit. The carers were very attentive. The residents seemed very happy. There was a wall chart which showed all the weekly activities and the bedrooms were spacious, bright and clean. The communal areas were very well kept also. I was impressed. I called the HSE again and finally the fair-deal had been passed (a bit late, was my first thought but hay hoe it was sorted now).

Ger, came home with his family to see mam. She was over the moon. You see Ger and my dad had been extremely close. They had the same profession and he like my dad had all those years ago. He also spoke like my dad and had the same great sense of humour. Therefore… you guessed it my mam thought he was my dad. To say she was delighted was an understatement. Ger, Eimear and mams grandchildren and great grandchild would spend hours with her. Trying to help her remember who each of them were. Some minutes she would get clarity and remember them the next minute it was gone. These moments of clarity are the ones you hold so dear. We had brought up mams CD player so Ger could play her music and sing along with her. She sat there happily holding his hand, sometimes lost in her own memories of time gone by.

ON THE MOVE AGAIN

It was at the day before New Years' eve that I received a call to say there was a room in Kilcock and mam would be moved later that day. She was due to arrive at the nursing home at 5pm. We would not even have time to go to Marino to help pack her up. Her brother Andrew was visiting when this all came about and he assured me he would pack up all mams things and meet me in Kilcock. I couldn't catch my breath. No time to think straight. They were moving mam and that was it. This is something I learned about our wonderful country, if you are old, try not to get sick, because if you do, you will be passed around like a hot potato, no one wants to keep you for too long as you are taking up a bed. Shocking really to see our elders, our loved ones, the people who made this country what it is, treated like they are an inconvenience but in my opinion and from my experience, that is how it is.

I would just like to say at this point I know everything seems to be flying along, trust me it was. To give you an idea of time frame my mam fell in 18th November, and was in a nursing home by 30th December.

My sister in law, Eimear drove myself and Gerard, out to meet mam at the nursing home; neither of us could think straight our heads were in a spin. Declan would follow later with our children when mam was settled. We arrived to a lovely lady waiting for us. She told us mam had not arrived yet but was on her way. She handed me a handful of documents to be signed but said it was ok if I took them home to read over them.

Mam arrived. She looked so frail; this had knocked 50 shades from her face. She was pale and looked frightened. I was so angry, how could they put her through this. I had to calm down for her sake. I was never so happy to have my brother by my side as I was then. Mam saw him and her face lit up. "Oh thank god you're here Frank, (My Dad), I don't know where I am or what I did wrong, Where am I? " Ger just played along. A wonderful lady called Mary came to meet mam at reception. She greeted her with a huge smile and said "hiya Marie, We have been dying to meet you" I started to relax. They brought us to one of the communal rooms. It was like sitting in a big open plan room with a kitchen and sitting area all in one. Lamps were lit and it was very cosy. It was very homely, just what I had wanted for mam.

Mary made a cup of tea for us all. As much as mam looked like she had relaxed a little she never let go of Gers' hand. He just spoke nice and softly to her, telling her it was going to be ok.

A short while later Declan and the children arrived. Mam was delighted to see them. As soon as the children came in everyone could leave as far as she was concerned, she only had eyes for them. While they had more tea and biscuits, Nicole and I got an opportunity to see mams room. It was lovely. Bright, clean and spacious. Her brother, Andrew, had brought all mams clothes from the unit but they all had to be given into reception to be labelled and washed. Looking around mams room I knew I had to bring some things from home to make it hers. This was not a problem; I was told I could even bring in some furniture if I wanted in case mam had a favourite chair or anything. It was a comfort to know she was going to be in a lovely place that might just feel a little like home.

After tea, we brought mam to her room. She kept asking what she was doing here and did she do something wrong. We just kept telling her that it was like another part of the hospital and she was just there until her leg got better. This settled her a little. The carers asked us to leave the room while they got mam changed into her nightclothes. When we re-entered she was all tucked up in bed, half asleep already. She had had a long day and needed her rest. We told her to rest and we would see her in the morning. She closed her eyes and within minutes she was fast asleep. We reluctantly left her. Took myself and Nicole about 3 times before we actually left, we just kept peeking back in to make sure she was ok. She was.

For the 1st time in a very long time I slept well. I didn't think I would as I was hoping she was ok but with no worrying about her possibly falling and lying on the floor all alone, No worrying about her leaving the house and going for wander, No worrying about her possibly doing something that could cause her any harm, I dozed off into a lovely sleep.

I awoke early, refreshed, so I got up and headed to the nursing home so I could have breakfast with her. When I got there I was happy to see her up, dressed and in the dining area chatting up a storm. I was introduced to all the lovely ladies who shared her new home.

I then got to work setting up mams room to look a little more homely. I had brought a few of her favourite things from home. One was her lamp, my dad had bought it for her many years ago and she loved it. It's amazing what a simple lamp can do, straight away the place looked better, no more bright lighting, mam could relax with a nice soft glow. I put her plush blanket on her bed and another on the chair as a throw. In her window I placed her vase and filled it with flowers then along the ledge, framed pictures of her mam and dad, family and friends. On her nightstand I put her cd player, a nicely decorated box of tissues and a framed picture of my dad.

On her dressing table I put her brush, some more flowers and more framed pictures of all her family. It might sound like I was surrounding her in pictures, I was, she loved them and our family home was always full of them. Declan had made mam a wonderful album, filled with happy memories, a few months previous and I placed it in her nightstand.

After breakfast I helped mam into her room. The smile on her face had said it all. I had done it just right.

She wanted to look at all the pictures and wanted some music on so I obliged. We sat there listening to Sonny Knowles, looking at the pictures in the album and chatting until it was lunch time. Sonny Knowles had become mams absolute favourite artist in her Alzheimer's years. She would play the cd over and over again. So much, that Nicole bought her another one, out of her pocket money, in case anything happened to this one.

The carers came in and helped mam back into the dining area for her lunch. Meals times were always a little difficult with mam but now we were at a stage where she had great difficulty feeding herself. It broke my heart to watch her struggle. She would drop more than what went in her mouth. So I started to feed her. I, my sisters and mam's brother Andrew had done this on a few occasions in the hospital but it always hurt to watch. To see this strong independent woman pre Alzheimer's, having to be fed, I felt like I was taking away her dignity. But you know what, after a while I realized I wasn't, it was just another thing that had to be done so she wouldn't feel useless. She would often get frustrated at the fact the spoon or fork were not going the way they should and so, to her, it was easier just to stop eating. And that could just not be allowed to happen. I was amazed at how she willingly allowed me to feed her. I had always thought she would fight me on this but she didn't.

Now that mam was settled I could concentrate on getting the Enduring power of attorney put into place. This would allow me to make decisions that were best for mam. It would allow me, should I need to, sell the house. It would allow me to access money, again if I needed to. I was already a signatory on mam and dads for many years in the bank. This needed to be re-done when mam had to set up new accounts when dad passed away. Being a signatory allows you to have access to their bank accounts so you can pay bills etc. Which came in very handy when I had to set up a direct debit for the nursing home.

I went to mams solicitor and she started the process for me. The solicitor should guide you through all the steps don't worry. Six to Eight weeks later it was all done. I had the official document. Please be aware that you should never give this original document away, it must be kept very safe as you don't get a second one. I recommend you copy it a good few times and if people need to see the original you can show them but never let them keep it, just give them a copy. As I mentioned at the start of the book, if all the EPOA documents are sitting there from early on its makes life much easier down the line. And this is down the line.

MAM'S NEW HOUSEMATES

When you walk into an Alzheimer's units of a nursing home it can come as quite a shock. I had seen mam do some peculiar things on our journey but that was just one person. When you see 10 people all doing these things at the same time it can be quite over whelming. It took me a few weeks to get used to this. Some people never get used to it. I personally think that is why mam and her new friends had very little visitors that I could see, and I was there a lot. I think people can be afraid, they forget that their loved one is still in there; you just have to wait a while to see them. And it might be just a glimpse but they are there. I think they see a stranger in their loved ones body and that is very hard to deal with. It is also hard to watch some of the things they do, maybe they are embarrassed, I know I was at the very start of this journey but there is really no need to be. These lovely people are just at different places in their mind and as soon as you realise this you can enjoy being with them again. Enjoy their stories because at this stage most of them can be true you just haven't heard them before because they happened a very long time ago. But one thing I did notice was that they love company.

One of mams new housemates loved to collect things, not necessarily her own things, just things. She would wander from room to room collecting little odds and ends that took her fancy.

This is why it is so important to label or mark everything that your loved one has brought with them. I bought a permanent marker and marked everything from a little vase, lamps, to the back of photographs. This makes it so much easier for the carers to put all the things back where they belong when they find them.

Another lady, Mary, loved to shout, she would stand there giving out about everything. She also had a tendency to hike up whatever she was wearing on the bottom part of her body into what can only be described as if she was going for a paddle. Her skirt would be stuck into her nickers or her trousers would be shoved up like shorts. One day while myself and the children were there, this wonderful lady started shouting at an empty chair, she was giving out to whoever she saw something fierce. Nicole and Paul looked a little frightened and asked who she was talking to. I just told them she see's someone sitting there and that is who she is talking to. Paul said "I wouldn't like to be them, they are in big trouble, and whatever they did must have been bad ". It was right then I know my children would adapt to this situation and all it quirkiness very well.

Ethel another lively lady had something to say about everything. She would constantly give out to the carers, they were always doing it wrong in her eyes and her favourite word was "No". I came to really like this lady, she was such a lovely person when you got to know her a little and took the time to talk to her she was really sweet. I used to agree with them all the whole time, so much easier. This lady would love to help. She would go around the kitchen, moving everything, taking out all the cups and glasses, forks and spoons and leaving them on the sideboards. She would often spill her tea onto the floor to feed the invisible cat at her feet.

Then there was Seamus, he was the image of father jack from the program "father Ted". He was never drunk but he would F & blind out of him. But when you spoke to him he was such a sweet gentleman. He would kindly request certain things and when you helped him he was very grateful and always thanked you sincerely.

One of the gentlemen, James, used to relax by lying on the floor, seemingly he had done this many years ago to relax himself before he went on stage. The carers would try and get him to sit on a chair but he would always slink back onto the floor. One day He lay on the floor right next to Declan's feet and started pulling on the ends of his trousers. Declan just smiled and said they were the only trousers he had and he'd have to get his own pair.

Betty was a voluptuous woman who had lived on a farm. She was extremely loud and took a disliking to mam for some reason. She would shout across the table, for no reason I might add, at mam. Saying that mam was a liar. Mam did not like that and she turned and said "Excuse me, I am not a liar" then added, "will someone please move her off this table she is too loud, it's out in the field she should be." Mam never knew she was a farmer. The woman just turned with a barrage of foul language and was moved. Mam took this one as a win. This woman was moved permanently to another area that was better suited to her.

Sally would shuffle around the halls, muttering to herself, often in her bare feet. No matter what the carers would do they could not keep slippers or shoes on her. Her hair used to fall around her face as she hung her head. It was quite a frightening sight, even for me someone who doesn't scare easily. Then they cut her hair in a lovely bob, and it opened up her face. She was lovely but she too liked to claim bits and bobs from other people's room. She once had her thumbs together and her hands in a choke hold position and was making a bee line for my mam. I know she wouldn't hurt her but Nicole was not so sure and put her arm securely around her nannies shoulders and made sure she was going to be between them. No-one was going to touch her nanny.

Over the months that followed mam found herself a best friend. She was wonderful lady, Victoria, who had lived in the same area mam had, when she was growing up. They had even gone to the same school. Only problem was she called mam "Margaret" but mam always answered so it wasn't really an issue. I often wondered if they had known each other back then because to look at them sitting there chatting, you would swear they had been friends all their lives. It was quite possible that they had. This lady had no family really to speak of, she was never married and had no children and her parents were long since gone. So we as a family always took time to have a little chat with her. My children always went around all the ladies and gave them a hug every time we left. To see how much joy it brought these ladies was wonderful to watch. Even the most stern would weaken with their hug.

OUR VISITS AND THE LITTLE STORIES

Every time Declan would visit, mam would shine. They would have a good old banter between them. She would constantly ask him "why won't you marry me?" He would try to explain that he was married to me, her daughter. She would scoff and say "that's only an excuse". Sometimes Declan's answers would change and he would tell her that of course he would marry her. She would be pleased with this answer... for all of 5 minutes. This was continuous, every day, same question, sometimes different answers, but he never got frustrated with her and just played the game.

On one of these occasions mam didn't ask Declan to marry her. When we went in she did not look too pleased to see us. She turned to Dec and said "I loved you but then you fecked off and married someone else". "Your daughter" was Dec's reply but she told him not to be so stupid he couldn't marry her daughter, she was only a little girl. He just agreed and said he was sorry. She still had a bit of an odd look in her eye but the children started singing with her and she soon forgot all about it.

It was my Birthday and I decided to mention it to mam. She asked me who my parents were. I said "you and dad are". She smiled, and said "who's your dad?" I replied "Frank". She took to laughing and said "Frank was not your father". I just

laughed and said "well it's a bit late telling me that now, as I can't even ask you who my real dad is as you won't remember ".
I didn't realise anyone was listening but everyone took to laughing. We must have laughed for about 5 minutes, you know one of those times when you just can't stop.

One evening, Mary was trying to wander into mams room. Mam was in the bathroom with the carers and Declan stood at the door, kind of like a body guard. He tried to guide the lady away but she wasn't having it. She wanted to get into the room. Declan just stood in the doorway. With that she punched him in the stomach and started shouting at him, saying "don't you dare hit me, i'll get my Johnny after you". Poor Declan nearly died his eyes were darting around looking for someone who could be a witness to say he hadn't touched her. I and one of the carers had been watching the whole event unfold. We were amused, Declan not so much. As we were leaving a while later, the same lady passed us with a big smile and said "night night love". Declan was mumbling under his breath but he soon got over it and saw the funny side.

Maureen would visit with mam often, but I could see how it would break her heart. Every time she would visit it was amazing, you would see a little glimpse of mam, she would remember her. She would always greet her with "ah there is my best friend" and give her the most glorious smile. Maureen would spend the time talking with mam and singing her old favourite-sonny Knowles. When we would leave I would always feel a little upset as I would see a tear in both their eyes. She would notice mam's deterioration at lot more than Me., as I was the one visiting every other day and you don't really notice it. But she did, she was watching her friend of 55 years fade before her very eyes and it hurt like hell.

As always I bought mam flowers every week. I loved the way it would brighten her up but I also noticed how it would brighten up the other ladies too but I never saw fresh flowers around. So I decided to go to Ikea, buy a few small vases and buy some little bunches of flowers for the other ladies in mams unit. Well I could have handed them a million pounds and I don't think I would have gotten a better reaction. I handed out the bunches, allowing each lady to pick whatever colour took her fancy. Then the carers would help them to place each of the little bunches into their vase. They now could have them in their own room or leave them in the seating area where they spent a lot of time. They nearly all choose the latter. I was surprised at the stories they made up when asked where they got the flowers. Some would say they had picked them from their garden that morning, others would say my family gave them to me or my beloved had just dropped them in. I didn't care for just that small moment in time they were all happy. So began a new routine, flowers for everyone every second week.

The minute mam would see anyone she would say "ah look who it is, give us a kiss". It was very funny to watch some of the male caterers go a bright shade of red as she would try to kiss them as they dished out her dinner.

MAMS BIRTHDAY

It was a lovely sunny day in May but more importantly it was Mam's birthday. The carers had organised a lovely cream cake with candles all lit up. Everyone sat around the table and sang her Happy Birthday. She shone. She was like a little girl sitting there with all her pals, smiling from ear to ear. We had cake and a cup of tea while we listened and joined in to the playings of ...you guessed it... Sonny Knowles. Afterwards she was exhausted; she got very tired very quick these days and she needed a nap. I reckoned she might have lots of visitors later so she needed her rest. I was right, her brothers came to wish her a happy birthday and while we were all sitting around mams bed chatting amongst ourselves (which is terrible but happens all the time unfortunately) I noticed Nicole perched up in mams bed, snuggling into her. I watched Nicole as she was intently staring at her nanny's face. Mams eyes were closed and her head was nodding. Nicole told me afterward she reckoned mam was talking to dad in heaven. It was such a lovely thought that in this world of mayhem she had somewhere she could feel at peace.

Mam did not like lots of people around her talking; I think it was just too noisy for her. She would be delighted to see people come but was also glad to see them go especially if there were too many which wasn't often thank god.

After everyone left we had our own little cake in mams room with her. As we sang Happy birthday again she started to cry, turned to the children and said "I love you, will you stay with me" Nicole quickly said "yes of course I will nanny". It was tea time and mam was moved back into the dining room. I have to say the food looked delicious, rashers, sausages, pudding, chips, bread and tea. Nicole fed her and then we headed home, all wishing her sweet dreams as we left.

THE SELLING OF OUR FAMILY HOME

It was June that mam took another little down turn. I arrived up to the home to see her fast asleep in bed. As I sat there the doctor came in and asked me to step outside mams room. I didn't know what to expect. It wasn't too bad at all mam had a little urinary infection but was now on antibiotics for it. She was going to be more tired than usual. I went back into her and she woke up. She looked more frail than normal, she just nodded gave me a little smile and closed her eyes. I took out a book that I had brought and I started to read it to her. I think mam had only ever completely read one book in all her years, she never had time plus she could just never get into them. Myself I am an avid reader and rather than just sitting in the room looking at her in silence I thought this might break the silence in a nice way. It was, little did I know then how many books I would read to her before she passed.

I called my siblings and explained about mams illness. We also had to talk about mams finances they were dwindling fast and a decision had to be made. I spoke to the HSE again and they said if I sold mams house, paid off her life loan that she could be re-assessed and that would bring the costs down.

So that was our decision made, we would have to sell the house. This was a huge decision; we were going to be selling our childhood home. We all agreed it was for the best. So I got started. I called the estate agent and she came out to view the house. She reckoned it would sell very quickly as it was a nice sized semi, in a good area close to tons of amenities. She said she would come back in a couple days to take the photos and put up a sign. Our job now was to clear the house of all unnecessary clutter and display it as minimalist as possible.

The next couple of days were very hard, emotionally and physically. Myself, Declan and a few friends boxed up lots of mams things. The estate agent returned and took lots of photos. Mams house went up for sale that Friday. Monday morning I got a call from her with an offer well over the asking price. I called my siblings and we all agreed it could be sold at the price offered. If we had of had plenty of time to play around with, we could have held off hoping for a bidding war but we also had a life-loan interest noose around our necks. The longer we waited the more interest was being added.

So that was it mams house was sold. Audrey, Viv and Ger came home to help us clear out the house. It was going to be a hard job. We had 55 years of a house and home to be gone through. Every cupboard, wardrobe, box would have to be emptied. The attic, including the 5 x 80ltr boxes that we had stored away, all cleared. Every photograph, every envelope and greeting card would have to be searched as mam had a tendency to put money in them. And we did not have a lot of time to do it in. To say this was hard is an understatement it was an emotional roller coaster for us all.

As my siblings arrived a strange feeling was in the air. We all sat down, had some dinner together and a few drinks. We talked about the task that was ahead of us. I remember Ger saying he had a sickly feeling in his stomach all the way home and that he felt like he was going for an interview not coming home; we all understood exactly what he meant. We also had some great laughs as we looked at the photos or just reminisced about times that had passed. The days passed quickly... Our days were pretty much made up of the same thing each day, Wake up-clear out house-eat-visit mam-clear out house-eat-visit mam-have a glass of wine-sleep. We wanted to recycle as much of mams stuff as we could so all the bed clothes went to dogs trust. The crockery, delph, cutlery, teapots, jugs, sugar bowls, Christmas lights, ornaments, cushions all went out to mams nursing home. They were greatly received and it was wonderful to think mam would eat from her own plates and drink from her own cups, it was again just delivering a little bit of home to her. Her new friends could carry around mams cushions.

We all got to pick our own pieces, photographs, memories. I also got the greeting card collection, I don't think I will ever have to buy a card again. We sorted all her clothes, putting some by for mam in case she would need them and we donated the rest to the charity shop. We put whatever big furniture we had on a face book page, just saying it was free to a good home but needed to be collected as soon as possible. We distributed her garden flower pots to all her neighbours to remind each one of her and to say thanks for their friendship to mam. I know this is going to sound just awful and cold but we also choose her burial outfit. Mam had some really good clothes but she never got to wear them anymore and we wanted to pick something that she loved and looked beautiful in. We choose her favourite purple suit, I carefully wrapped it up and brought it to my house

On one occasion, as myself and Audrey were going into visit mam we were approached by the nurse. She asked if we could come into her office for a few minutes to answer a few questions. She explained that mams health was getting worse and she wanted to explain about what happens. She said that if mam ever needed it, they would assign a palliative care team. She asked if we had thought about funeral arrangements, had we picked a funeral home? Where was it? Was mam going to be buried or cremated? Thankfully I knew all of these answers as my mam and I had discussed these issues at length a long time ago. She just told me that you can never tell and she just wanted to be prepared now, rather than put me through these questions at a harder time. We understood and was actually a little relieved that they now had all mams wishes.

My sibling's time at home came to an end. As they each walked out of the house I could see the pain in their eyes. The only thing to remember was we were doing this to help mam. We were funding her new home. Her old home was going to have wonderful new life in it, a lovely couple, with their 2 children had bought mams house. I wished them every happiness.

OUR HOLIDAY

Now that mams house was gone, it was a little easier for us. We did not have to worry about people breaking into her home or the pipes getting frozen up in the winter. It would also mean we could cancel the insurance and all those little utilities that added up and drained mams account.

We had decided to take a holiday, we hadn't had one for a few years as we didn't want to leave her. Keith, Audrey's son was getting married in Hawaii and we really wanted to go. I knew mam was in good hands and for the first time in a long time I felt that I could relax and enjoy our much needed break.

Just before we headed off at the end of July, we all visited mam. She was in great form. I felt so guilty knowing I was not going to see her for a few weeks. Visiting her every other day had become a huge part of my routine. But I was assured by all the carers they would keep an extra special eye on her. I also contacted her brothers and asked them to please call in whilst I was away, that way she may not miss me. I know this sounds really silly as mam would have had no idea that I was even gone, but it made me feel a little better. I used to do that a lot, try to make myself feel less guilty. I know now there was no need to feel that way but that is easier said than done at the time. Mam's brothers, sisters in law and my cousin made sure that she wouldn't have time to miss me.

Whilst we were in the middle of our holiday, I got a call. Mam had taken a turn and was not well again. She had another urinary infection and they were putting her back on antibiotics. The guilt flooded over me. Should I head home? Should I stay? The doctor assured me that there was no urgency and to continue with my holiday. I did so with a heavy heart but tried to stay happy for everyone's' sake. I didn't even tell Audrey until after her sons' wedding, as I didn't want to ruin it for her. The flight home could not go quick enough. I tried to sleep in vain. I was hoping if I had enough sleep I would be able to drive straight out but that was not going to be the case. When we got home, we all headed to bed for a couple of hours and the minute I woke I was up and dressed ready to go.

When I entered mams room she looked worse than I had ever seen before. She was grey. The doctor came down to her room and explained this was really taking it out of her. I stayed in that room for hours; she never opened her eyes once. I talked to her, I read to her but I got no reaction, this was really worrying.

THE DREADED CALL

After a couple of days, mam started to look a little brighter. I know this is going to seem like I have forgotten lots of things but to be honest I don't want to bore you with my daily routine. For the next couple of months that I visited mam, some days she would be great, sitting up singing and chatting with her friends other days she would be in bed too weak to get up. I was told a long time ago that our elders often get weaker in the winter months. This is true. I noticed a good few of the residents go down-hill a little during this time. Mam was one of them

It was at the start of November I got my call. The doctor asked me to meet her A.S.A.P in the home. I rushed out the door, and broke every speed limit getting there. As I approached mams door the doctor came out. I knew by the look on her face this was bad news. She explained that mam had yet another infection. She said that the antibiotics were not working this time and mam was very weak and had a high temperature. She said that the next 48 hours were going to be very hard, and she didn't know if mam would have the strength to fight this one off. She said that at this stage mam could be put on a drip but normally this is only done for the family, it does not do anything really for the patient, it only prolongs her pain. I said there was no way I would out my mam through 1 minute pain if I could avoid it. I asked if I should call my siblings and she said she couldn't make that decision for me as she really didn't know.

I was shell shocked. I knew this day had been coming for a long time but I still wasn't ready for it. I numbly called Declan and told him what was happening; he said he would be up straight away. I called my sisters and brothers and repeated what I had just been told. I said I would keep them informed as the day went on.

As the day progressed mam did not get any better. She was mumbling and nodding a lot. Her temperature not lowering and she was in a lot of pain in her stomach. The nurses would give her paracetamol for it. I just sat there watching her face. The carers would pop in and out and say how sorry they were. They fed and watered me all day long. Day turned to night and there was still no change. I came home, had 5 hours sleep and went straight back up she was still the same. The hours ticked by, my sisters and brothers calling all the time, looking for an update. There was no change what could I say. Audrey called and said she had booked her flight and was coming home. I was so relieved that I didn't have to make that call and tell her that she should come home. She was so far away and the cost was incredible but as always she had my back.

Ger had just taken a new position in Poland and couldn't leave right at that moment and Viv had a family to think of in

France. It was a hard decision for people to make. There was no time limit on this. We didn't know if or when mam might decide to leave us.

We collected Audrey from the airport and went straight out to see mam. She could see how weak mam was and was glad she had come home. Mam had made it through the 48 hours. She was still fighting.

We were told that a lot of people take one last upturn before they go downhill for the last time. Mam held on, we thought she might be waiting on one of her children but as each of my siblings, Viv then Robert then Ger, arrived home mam rallied, she would lay there, singing, laughing, talking, and probably making the most sense that she had in the last year. Her mind seemed clear. This was astonishing, how could this be, I have to admit I felt really stupid and guilty. Here I was after calling them all home because I thought mam was going to pass and mam is singing with them. All I could do was enjoy the time. We still made sure everyone got to have their private moment with mam. For me this was the most important thing we could do right now. I did not want anyone to have any regrets. So every daughter, son, sons in law, daughters in law, grandchildren and great grandchild had our own special time alone with mam. Saying everything we had on our minds, letting her know how much she was loved and how it was ok to go. I had done a little research on people who were dying and over and over I read how all you can do is repeatedly tell them that it is ok to go, so that they do not feel bad leaving their loved ones behind. Mam was very responsive to us and everyone walked away feeling that they had had a real connection with her.

But something was holding her here. We had no idea what. She kept saying she was waiting on Frank or The little girl. She would tell us that dad, and her mam and dad were in the room on a daily basis. At first this seemed a little odd but as the days turned into weeks we just accepted the fact that maybe mam could see things that we couldn't and would just say "Hi Dad".

Even though mam was at deaths door her sense of humour and dry wit was still alive and kicking. As Nicole would sit up beside her in the bed mam would whisper to her saying things like "what are they all doing here, do they think I'm going to get up and do the hokeycokey or something" Or " come on love lets me and you get out of here these are all driving me mad". One day Viv asked mam where frank was and mam replied that he had been there a few minutes ago but the shagger had fecked off with some other woman.

Declan called her favourite priest and explained mam's situation and asked him if he would come see mam. He kindly agreed to come out the very next day. The next day as we all stood around mams bed praying, mam said every prayer, not missing a word. He blessed mams forehead and she had the most peaceful look on her face.

Not long after the priest left Viv wiped mams forehead and said "that bit of sweat was annoying me". We told her she had just wiped away mam VIP pass into heaven that, that sweat, was the anointing oil. She was mortified.

Mam couldn't eat anymore and was only drinking water. Her internal problems were a lot worse and she couldn't be fed as the food would only make her sick and cause her immense pain in her tummy. These were rollercoaster days. One day she would be chatting the next you would not get a word, one day she would have a little colour in her face the next she was grey. She couldn't really move anymore, even turning her head had become a mountainous effort. The pain was definitely getting much worse.

We spoke to the doctor about mams pain management. She said they would have mam on a baseline of morphine but that if we noticed that she was in pain just to tell the nurse and she could be given something. Knowing how busy the staff were we knew this was going to be down to us to watch out for mam. My brother and sisters took turns to sleep up in the nursing home. You see mam's pain would get extremely bad but unless you were sitting in the room 24-7 you could easily miss it. On a couple of occasions my normally very docile brother, Gerard, had to lose his rag in order to get mam some pain relief and was not happy leaving mam alone as he felt she might get over looked. Mam was never an attention seeker and rather than scream in pain, like most people would (I know I would) her face would scrunch up and all she could let out was a faint Ohhhhhhh.

The nurse would be contacted and on the majority of times mam would be given something straight away. Unfortunately this is where the system fails a little. We were not doctors or nurses we were just children seeing their mother in pain and wanted it to stop. On occasion, we would have to wait long periods of time before someone would come to give her something. I remember one night in particular as Viv and I sat there, mam started to cry with the pain. Viv ran down to the nurse's station and told them. 15 minutes later mam was still in pain so Viv went down again. They said they would get someone straight down. It was only after the 3rd time and Viv threatening to call the doctor and go searching for the administering nurse herself that the nurse came in. She rudely said that mam was probably only trying to talk. I flipped and told her if she waited a few minutes she would see for herself how much pain mam was in. She just shrugged her shoulders and left saying ok she would get something. I was so mad I even recorded my mam crying out in pain on my phone so I could shove it where the sun doesn't shine when she came back in. But when she arrived back she was as nice as pie, I couldn't believe it. Thankfully this nurse was only a stand in and not the regular nurse but we had to try and find a solution as we did not want mam to suffer in any way.

We called a hospice and explained what was happening but as much as they would have loved to help they did not take Alzheimer's patients. It felt so unfair. I knew the hospice was amazing as they had cared for my father all those years ago and he was never in an ounce of pain. What could we do now? We arranged to meet with the manager of the home and the doctor and told them exactly what was happening. This seemed to work. They did something because after that as soon as we told someone mam was in pain they were quick off the mark.

THE MYSTERIOUS E-MAIL

Even though mam was extremely ill that did not stop her new found friends dropping by. This was frustrating at times because emotions were high and when you see someone trying to walk off with your mams things as she is lying there helpless you had to try to be patient. We would just guide them back out of mams room as quickly and pleasantly as we could. The carers recommended we lock the door when we were in there so we could have our time with mam and should they need to come in they would simply knock. We were very grateful of this solution. So that's what we started to do.

This solution did not suit everyone as it seems, as a few days later we got a call from HIQA (Health Information and Quality Authority) Audrey took the call. The lady on the other end asked to speak to mam. Audrey explained that mam was bed ridden and would not be able to talk to her. The lady proceeded to tell Audrey that they had an email supposedly from mam and the contents concerned them enough to make a call. Audrey explained that mam was dying and that there was no way possible that mam could have written it. I have to add here my mam never owned a computer in her life, she would not have known how to turn it on, let alone send an email. The HIQA lady apologised and asked if we were happy with the care mam was being given. Audrey told her that everything was grand now and the carers were fantastic, which they were by the way. She said she would be in touch with the home manager, so were we.

Cutting a very long story short. After going back and forth between the home and HIQA, threatening law suits, we got a copy of the email. It basically said that we were locking mam in a room and not allowing any staff access to her. We were starving her and we were all just sitting around her bed watching her, waiting on her to die. It also claimed we were trying to overdose her with medication and would someone please come and save her.it also stated that other residents were being starved and left dehydrated like her. I have to say none of this was the case that I witnessed anyway. I have to reiterate here that this was meant to have been written by my mam. Someone, a disgruntled temporary employee I reckon, had gone and set up an email address for my mam and had written this disgusting letter. There was a huge mix of emotions, anger, confusion, sadness and then even more anger. I just wanted to kill whoever had written this letter. Here we were watching our mother die and someone, who definitely did not know the full circumstances, thought it was ok to pretend to be her and add to our emotional turmoil.

I would just like to say that the carers always had looked after the residents with care and made sure their every need was looked after, maybe they could have had a little more help every now and again as they were permanently rushed off their feet, but they never showed this to the residents, and trust me at this stage I was practically a resident myself.

The manager of the home said they had called a meeting and had given the staff member 2 days to come forward no one did. The matter was and is still now with the Garda.

ON OUR OWN AGAIN AND LITTLE PIECE OF ADVICE

Over the next Month, My siblings had to return to their own homes. This was very difficult for them but they couldn't stay indefinitely and mam was not ready to take her place in heaven yet. So again it was just us.

I would sit by her bed reading to her, singing to her and talking to her day after day, myself and Declan taking it in shifts. One day when I arrived up Sally was sitting in the chair beside mam. On mams chest was a few chocolates. Sally was sharing mams chocolates with her. Five for Sally, one for mam. It was so lovely to see. As I came in she got up from the chair, fixed mams bed clothes, told me that mam was not well and left the room. I discarded the chocolates and took my seat. As I sat there a few more residents dropped by to say hi. A new gentleman had arrived, Pauric, and it was so lovely to see the little budding romance between himself and Victoria. They would sit together on a couch and have little chats. The lady and the gentleman. One day when my children were in. Nicole went into the main room and was chatting with the residents. They loved the attention they got from the children. Nicole arrived back in mams room in fits of laughing stating that Pauric had offered her a Jaunt around the home in a wheelchair, He reckoned it would be great fun, Nicole thought so too but decided against it for fear of getting into trouble.

Day to day would be different, again on the emotional roller coaster. Some days she would be good other days she would be really bad. She often just stared at the ceiling and spoke to loved ones that had gone before. She would chat to them for quite long periods of time and it seemed as though she couldn't hear me at time, it was that or she was just ignoring me.

As I sat there one evening a wonderful lady, who also visited the home, dropped by to see me. She had often dropped by to see how mam was doing Over the past year we had built up our own little friendship. She gave me a fantastic piece of advice and I shall pass it onto you. She hoped she wasn't being too personal but asked if I had access to mams money. I was a bit cautious, although I'd no reason to be, and said that I had. She then told me that if I could, I should withdraw mams funeral costs now because if I didn't mams money could easily get frozen until her will was sorted out and this could take a couple of years. She had known someone who had to take out a personal loan to pay for their parents' funeral because all their parents' assets were frozen as the will went into probate. I never knew any of this I thanked her dearly and promised I would check it out. She just didn't want me having to fork out money that I didn't have.

I did and I discovered that because mam was now essentially the last woman standing in her marriage, if she had more than €12,000 between her bank accounts and assets, her will would have to go to probate. This would mean we would either have to put it to probate ourselves or the solicitor could do it for us but either way it would go to the courts and by the time the whole thing would be completed it could take years before any money would be released. Under some circumstances, depending on the bank, they may release the funeral cost when shown the relevant invoice. And they may even release some money for "the afters" but again this is not a definite.

I called the funeral home and asked them the approximate cost of funerals they gave me a ball park figure. I called mams favourite eatery and asked for an approximate cost there too. I totalled the two and I knew myself or my siblings would not have that kind of money so I called my sisters and brother and Ok'd a withdrawal of the money. I didn't hang around the next day I withdrew the approximate funds and held in a safe place. If it was anymore at least we could gather that together between us. I was relieved that this was all sorted and could now go back to enjoying my time with mam without worrying about be able to afford to fulfil mams wishes.

Mam would say very odd things at times. One day in particular she was extremely confused and while we were in the middle of chatting and I said "Fr Paul was asking for you" to which she said "Who's that", I explained he was her favourite priest she asked what's a priest ? I again explained and she answered with "Who's God?" I was gobsmacked; I couldn't believe she had forgotten who God was. She continued this line of confusion with stating that she had no idea who Frank was, and she had no children, and she never smoked (which was true she never smoked a day in her life). She kept saying she had to get out of here but she couldn't leave until Christmas. I turned on her old favourite Sonny Knowles to try rest her mind a little but was told to turn him off she didn't like him, so it was x-factor winner, Mary Byrne's, job to sing mam into a nice relaxed state. She succeeded; mam closed her eyes and smiled. She was at ease again.

Her feet and hands would get so cold they would have to put layers of blankets on the bed to try keep her warm. They never warmed up very much at all regardless of the amount of layers.

At this point mam was just a slip of a person. She had not eaten in 6 weeks and her face was tiny. She had lost so much weight that while Ger was there she decided to spit out her false teeth as they didn't fit properly anymore. Poor Gerard nearly passed out with the fright. He put them in a glass in the bathroom, I found out later this was a big mistake.

One day I decided to clean her teeth only to discover an empty glass. Where were her teeth? While mam was resting I went and asked one of the carers had they seen mams teeth, she, like me thought they were in the bathroom. She promised she would ask everyone and try and find them. The thought of where these teeth might be, amused me. The image of Sally walking in with 2 sets of dentures in nearly made me fall off the chair laughing. I don't know if it was tiredness or just lack of laughter in my life at that moment but the images kept coming, maybe they would find one of the dolls or teddies with a new set of dentures. I was having a fit of the giggles when one of the carers came in to apologise about the missing teeth and when I explained why I was laughing she soon joined me. By the time we were finished giggling mams room had about 5-6 people , carers and residents, all laughing our heads off, each proposing a new place the teeth might appear. We never did find her teeth.

Mams base line for her morphine was being increased weekly, which was really helping to keep mam nice and comfortable. It was during the last couple of weeks in December that communication from mam was almost gone. She no longer smiled, her eyes closed nearly all of the time. It was really hard to see her breathing at times. She would try to talk but all that came out was an inaudible whisper.

NEARING THE END

Christmas day arrived and we headed up to see mam first thing. She was just lying there in an almost comatose state. The children sang lots of Christmas carols to her but we did not get any response. Nicole and Paul went into the main room and stood there singing their hearts out, much to the delight of everyone there. It was a sad day. We went home and cooked dinner; it just did not seem right, mam lying in a bed and us here enjoying dinner without her. It was a long day. There was no change with mam

A couple of days later when I tried to give mam some water she almost choked. One of the carers tried to make me feel better by informing me that it had happened to her earlier that morning too. Mam was also suffering from dreadful thrush in her mouth, the carers managed to treat it. Over the last while mam could at least take water from a straw but now she did not have the strength to suck it up. I was now at the stage that all mam could do was give a tiny suck on a watered sponge. It was the day before New Year's, (mams one year anniversary of being in the nursing home) that the nurse told me mam had deteriorated more. Her breathing had changed it was now fast and heavy on the heart and the infection now seemed to be on the chest. They said they would be on extra watch and would contact me straight away if anything happened. One of the carers asked me if it was at all possible to get a pure white night dress as this is what they liked to put on those who had passed. I thought it was a lovely gesture.

I thought getting a plain white nightdress was going to be a very simple task but it proved to be a very difficult one. I found white with spots, stripes, patterned even but no plain white. I tried all the usual suspects, Dunnes, Pennys, Marks, Guineys, Boyers, anywhere I thought might have a nice age appropriate night dress but no luck. After visiting almost every shop in the city centre I almost gave up and then I remembered Debenhams. It was my lucky day I found 1 white nightdress at the back of lots of others. It was mams size, so I whipped it up and brought it to the till. The girl said she hadn't seen this nightdress before and had no idea where it came from but it had a tag on it so she sold it to me. I was never so happy to have a granny nighty in my hands. I guarded it like it was the crown jewels until I got it up into mams wardrobe.

Of all the years of living with Alzheimer's this had to have been the hardest time. Before I could always work out the things that were bothering mam but now she couldn't tell me she couldn't even give me a hint. I never felt so useless, helpless and it killed me. All my poor siblings were texting constantly waiting on some news all I could do was tell them how she was at that moment. It was as frustrating for me as it was for them. I have to be honest I did get inappropriate at times as the texts felt like a copy and paste moment, for example. Viv had text me asking how mam looked and I replied with "like she is going to a party" completely inappropriate but I got my little giggles where I could.

The doctor came in and agreed it wouldn't be too much longer. She even said that mam had re-written the book on this. Mam could no longer suck and all we could do was wet her lips with a cotton swab. Her breathing kept changing, fast and hard to slow and soft. She also had a temperature. But at least she was comfortable. As each of the carers dropped in I could see it in their eyes that they noticed it too. They would each walk out with tears welling up in their eyes.

I decided to speak to the manager and get a heads up of what the protocol is when the time actually comes. She explained to me that the doctor is called to pronounce it then they contact the coroner, explain the illness and then he decides on an autopsy or a release. Then we had to contact the funeral home who would come out and take mam for preparation.

Audrey arrived home new years' day. We headed straight up to the home. Audrey then basically camped next to mams bed for the next 2 days. She slept, or should I say stayed there 24 hrs a days. At this stage I just couldn't do it anymore. I had finally reached my breaking point. I had watched my mam dying for the last 8 weeks but now that her breathing had all changed, I just couldn't listen to her dying. So my visits were less frequent and thank god Audrey took my place, it eased my guilt. Mam stayed the same for the next couple of days.

On the 3rd of January I went up and saw my poor exhausted sister sitting there. Mam was no different. I explained to Audrey that if mam had wanted to go while she was there she would be with the angels by now. But Audrey would need her strength for what was coming next. After a lot of discussion Audrey agreed to come home for a few hours to sleep and have a shower. We would go back up in the evening.

A NEW ANGEL GETS HER WINGS

While Audrey slept I decided I needed to take down my Christmas decorations. I would need the space and it was time anyway. The children and I got to work and a couple of hours later, Audrey woke feeling a little rested. Declan and I loaded the van with some of the Christmas decoration boxes and went on our 1st trip to our storage unit. Just as we were approaching the house on our return my phone rang. I looked at the ID, it was the nursing home, my heart sank. I answered. "I am terribly sorry Ruth but your mam has passed away". The words spun around in my head, my heart dropped but at the same time relief overflowed. She was finally at peace, no more pain, no more confusion. She was with my dad, the place she had wanted to be for the past 6 years. Declan knew straight away. We pulled up to the house and Declan called Nicole and Paul outside to tell them. I walked into the sitting room to see Audrey standing on the chair taking down the crib from the top of the cabinet. I asked her to get down. "She's Gone" was all I could get out without both of us bursting into tears. Nicole and Paul came in and we all just stood hugging each other. Paul then turned to Audrey and said "Does that mean Terry can come now?" Audrey started to laugh and said "yes it does". Afterwards she told me that Paul had been wondering when Terry, Audrey's husband, and was coming back and she had told him that he wouldn't be able to come back until nanny's funeral. Trust Paul to be keeping it real.

They had learned just to get on with things. You see my children had been through a whole lot in the past few years. I kind of took it for granted really. Their personal feelings and needs were sometimes put aside to deal with bigger issues with mam. They had been shifted in and out of their beds, onto blow up beds etc. When people would descend on us. They would have to be up for school every morning even though the house had been full of people chatting until the early hours. They would have to try and get their homework done with mam constantly asking them questions when I would be cleaning my mams house. They would be refused a dog because I didn't have the time to look after it and mam. They would have to do little dances' while they waited for me to bleach the bathroom before they could go because mam had had another "accident". They would have to answer the same questions over and over and over again but never once lost their patience. I'd apologise often but they would just say "its ok mam you have to make sure nanny is ok we don't mind". They made me so proud, still do.

Declan was crestfallen at the news. You see he had always agonised about mam going into a nursing home. When dad was on his death bed, Declan promised him that he would look after mam. I'm sure at the time he had no idea what was going to be involved, any other man would have run for the hills by now. But not Declan, He had looked after mam all through the years. He had made sure she was safe. Had made sure she wanted for nothing and was involved in everything. He had kept her company, he had held her hand when she was scared, he had taken her to her hospital appointments and MRI scans. He had put his time and business on the line to make sure mam never wanted or needed anything. We have our own small business which struggles at times because of larger companies trying to squash us. But Declan never made mam feel she was being an inconvenience when she or I would call because there was a problem that I couldn't manage myself. He did all of this not only because he had promised dad but because he loved her. And with that she loved him.

After the news had sank in a little we got to calling everyone, the same reaction going across the board, sadness but relief for mam. We got ready quickly and headed up to the nursing home.

When we arrived we were met with such understanding. The carers had moved all the residents to the other communal seating area and had given us the use of the entire main room and kitchen. We entered mams room, for the first time in weeks she looked peaceful. Strangely her hair looked younger, less grey. One of her eyes couldn't close completely and she looked like she was giving us a little wink, or maybe she was still keeping her eye on us.

We each said a little prayer, a goodbye and I wished her a safe journey to dad. After a while we into the main room and one of the carers brought us in a pot of tea, some sandwiches, biscuits and a small pot of hot chocolate for the children. The Christmas tree lights, in the corner, gave off a lovely soft glow. Even though this was such a sad time I was so glad we had picked this nursing home for her. It had always been so warm and homely and right now I was much happier sitting in that room than in a hospital. The staff couldn't do enough for us.

As we waited for the doctor to arrive to pronounce mam, Paul needed to use the bathroom so I asked Declan to bring him into mams room and stay with him so he wouldn't be scared. As the time slipped by I completely forgot Why Declan was in there and called him to answer a question I had. All our minds were so muddled that we all forgot Paul was still in the bathroom. Dec ran in only to find Paul standing next to mams bed, chatting away to her. It just proved to me that my children had a very special relationship with their nanny and they too were ready for her to go to heaven. He was not even a little bit scared, "why should I be", he said," its only nanny".

A doctor we had not seen before came, a short while later and said all was ok. The girls then went into mams room and prepared her. To this day I don't know how they did it. They were fantastic. They had so much respect for mam and treated her with such dignity.

When we re-entered mam was all laid out. The room was very elegant, mams lamp was on and her flowers were displayed on her bedside table alongside it stood a cross. She looked beautiful. Her hair was brushed and her eyes finally completely closed and they had even managed to put a little smile on mams face. We all relaxed a little and Paul turned and said "hey nanny's smiling now how did she do that". It was so sweet and funny at the same time.

When do you leave your loved one after they have passed the time just never seemed right but we had the children with us and we all needed to sleep. We had a lot to do.

THE REMOVAL

The following day we had arranged to meet the funeral directors that afternoon. They would collect mam at 12.00 noon. We wanted to be there.

We arrived a little early and started to sort through mams things. I know this might seem really cold but to be honest I had decided that when I left there I was not coming back. I did not want to visit somewhere that my mam would not be.

We bagged up her precious photos, albums, handbag, CD player and other little bits and bobs and placed them in the car. We asked the carers and the manager to give mams lamp to Victoria as she still only had a main light in her room. Mams vases could be put into the main area and her clothes could be passed on if they so wished. I couldn't believe how grateful they were for the clothes, they said a lot of residents do not have family that can bring them in clothes so with that I headed out to the car and brought in my "stash bag". It was a bag of brand new clothes and socks, just in case I noticed mams clothes getting a little worn. They were delighted.

As we stood in mams room waiting for the funeral men one of the carers came up and said Audrey was wanted at reception. Off she went and when she returned she had a face like a bull. The gentlemen had been there but because the doctor was not there to sign their form they could not take mam.

The staff tried to get the doctor; she was not available to come down but had also said she was not aware that mam was being cremated. I had told the nurse all that time ago but she said she knew nothing. She said if they left the form she would sign it later. The gentlemen called the office to see if this was ok and only because the lady there knew the family she said it was.

The gentlemen came into mams room with a new nurse that I had never met. She started saying mam needed to be dressed and making a huge deal about it. The guys said mam was fine that her clothes would be put on her after she was embalmed. I honestly thought Audrey was going to lose it. Finally the gentlemen convinced the nurse they knew exactly what they were doing and mam was finally able to leave the room.

Just as she being wheeled out of her room one of the carers came over to me and said that they normally turn off the music but because mam loved music so much would they leave it on. I said that that would be a lovely idea; I don't think I could have bared the silence if I'm honest.

As they began their walk down the corridor a song blasted out of the cd. "Wish me luck as you wave me goodbye" sang by Gracie Fields. As I listened to the words and as the tears flows down my face, I smiled. Trust mam to put a smile on my face at a time like this.

As we followed the coffin to the doors, the corridors were lined with the staff. All blessing themselves and saying a little goodbye as she passed. It was beautiful; she had received a guard of honor. As we were arrived at the door I gave each of mams carers a big hug and thanked them for being so kind to mam and I.

As we headed down the M50 we watched as the hearse went one way and we had to turn for home.

That afternoon we met with the funeral directors. We thanked her for helping us at such an emotional time and promised we would make sure they got that form quickly. We sorted out all the arrangements with such ease, it was almost too easy but I knew exactly what mam wanted and nothing was a problem.

Over the next 24 Hours Audrey spent most of the day arguing with the home because the doctor had still not brought over the form. We also needed the doctor's letter so we could get mams death certificate. Eventually and after a lot of running around, the funeral home got their form and we got the death cert.

MAM'S WAKE

As all my family arrived home, brothers, sisters, brothers in law, sisters in law, nieces, nephews and great nephew the house felt the happiest it had been in a long time. We all sat there telling our favorite stories of mam.

We still had to decide on the songs for the church and crematorium. As we went through the list picking the church songs was easy. We had mams songs picked out in no time. Then came the crematorium songs we needed two. One for as we enter and one for when the curtains closed.

Audrey and I very rarely row we are normally on the same page and to be fair she was pretty much letting me run the show (can't think of a better way to put it). But when I suggested a song she put her foot down, there was no way I could have that song. She kept picking all the lovely slow ballads that mam so loved but I thought when we were leaving the nursing home mam was sending me a message.

So every time Audrey walked in or out of a room I kept playing "Wish me luck as you wave me goodbye". We would all laugh ourselves silly and with everyone humming the tune even when it wasn't playing I knew I had her. She came to me with a compromise. I could have it but only if it was the Vera Lynn version, I quickly agreed.

If you have never really listened to this song before you should, the words are a perfect way to say goodbye to someone, well at least I thought so. And on the day of mams funeral everyone else thought so too. As the curtains closed and the tears flowed, a smile was on peoples' faces too. Mam would be proud she hated seeing anyone sad.

As we left the crematorium the amount of people that told me that it was a wonderful send off and the song at the end was "So Mam" was astounding. She had sent me her final message and I had heard her loud and clear.

Mams funeral pretty much took on a life of its own. The ballad sessions went on for 3 days. By the time it was all over I was exhausted, emotionally and physically.

A NEW CHAPTER

I guess this is where the story ends. The only problems that arose after were the unexpected bills or phone calls. Every couple of months, just as I was moving on a little, I would get some kind of post for mam from the chemist, the home or the HSE. That one was a good one I got a form, 6 months after mam had died, requesting a schedule of Assets (form CA24) and for it to be filled in asap. Why so urgent now? I asked myself. But I completed all the necessary forms and went to all the meetings regarding mams will. It is now finally all complete, I hope

It is now time for a new chapter in my life. We have since gotten 2 dogs and the children, although they still miss their nanny, talk about her often. Pictures of her flood our home.

I guess that's the whole reason I wrote this book is I needed to put to rest the thoughts and questions that still rolled around in my head. Had I done the right thing putting her in a home? Had I looked after her enough? Was she happy? I can now honestly say that all I did was my best. I loved mam with all my heart and would have done anything for her. Over the time we shared we laughed, we cried, we argued, we hugged but mostly we just spent time together. Of all the things mam needed, the biggest thing of all was us spending time with her, loving her the same way we always had, never letting that horrible disease make me forget who she really was.

I think that is one of the hardest things during the whole process remembering that your loved one is still in there. They have not gone away they have not been taken over by aliens, although sometimes it feels like that. They still love you. I think this disease scares people; they don't know what to do or how to react. Don't be afraid of who they are, enjoy their company as you have always done, just be patient and remember it's not about you, it's about them. It's a whole lot scarier for them than it is for you. You know who they are, sometimes they may not know you, you could be a stranger standing in their home. They are confused and often feel very lonely because they have lost a whole lot more than you have.

I hope you enjoyed reading this and you are not closing the cover saying, "well that was a waste of time". If you have someone who if suffering from the disease just remember you are not alone. There are many people out there going through the exact same thing as you are. Remember its ok to laugh. Just do your best and I hope this has given you a little Heads Up On Alzheimer's.

ABOUT THE AUTHOR

My name is Ruth Colgan. I was born and raised in Finglas. I am married to a wonderful man and have two beautiful children. I have two brothers and two sisters, who have all emigrated. I have two dogs who are members of our family.

Made in the USA
Middletown, DE
03 April 2024

52528586R00076